W9-AAP-753

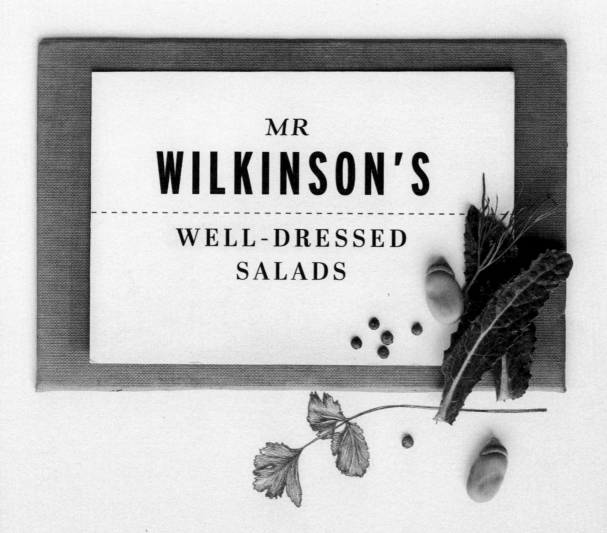

MR
WILKINSON'S
WELL-DRESSED
SALADS

SOUTH PARK TOWNSHIP LIBRARY
2575 Brownsville Road
South Park, PA 15129
(412) 833-5585

MR
WILKINSON'S

WELL-DRESSED
SALADS

SOUTH PARK TOWNSHIP LIBRARY
2575 Brownsville Road
South Park, PA 15129
(412) 833-5585

06   2015

BLACK DOG
& LEVENTHAL
PUBLISHERS
NEW YORK

DEDICATION

I close my eyes and I think of you all,
my heart beats faster and is full of love.
Thank you Sharlee, our two little hooligans Finn
Thomas & Jay Thomas, and yes even you Quincy.

X X X.

CONTENTS

THANK YOU

Before you read on, I would like to say thank you
for picking my book up. In a time when there are so many
cookbooks out there, it's amazing that you have taken the time
to read, buy, or just even flick through this one.

I hope you enjoy my thoughts on all things salads and a
love of food I share with my family.

WILKIPEDIA

Salad: A marriage of flavors & textures that you bring together, that does not have a food group or category.

Salad Dressing: A sauce used to dress the above.

Well Dressed: - the balance of dressing on your salad, so the two are in harmony together.

- the memory of my grandfathers, Tom & Bob, always clothed so smartly.

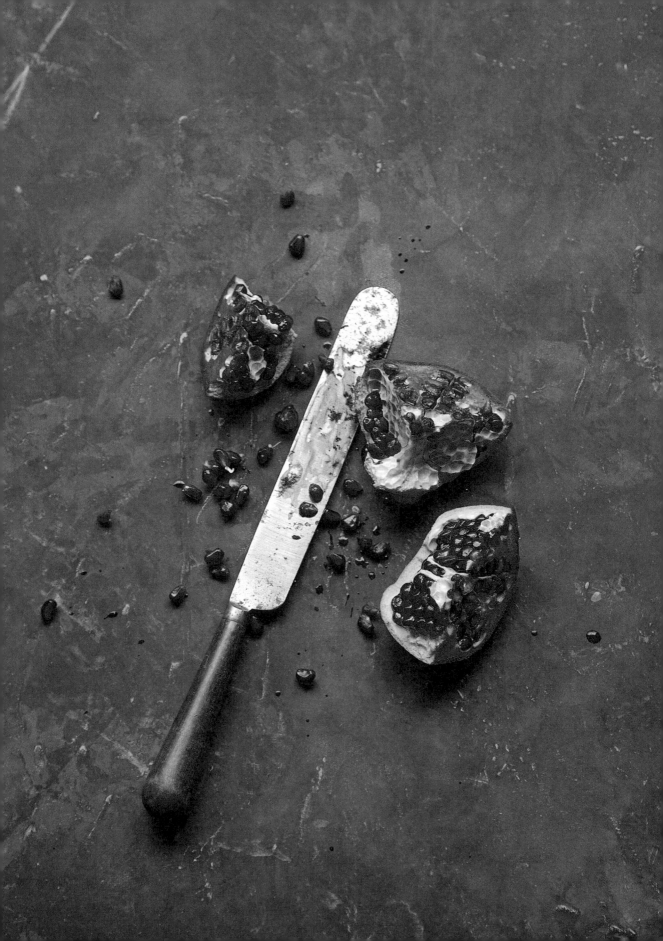

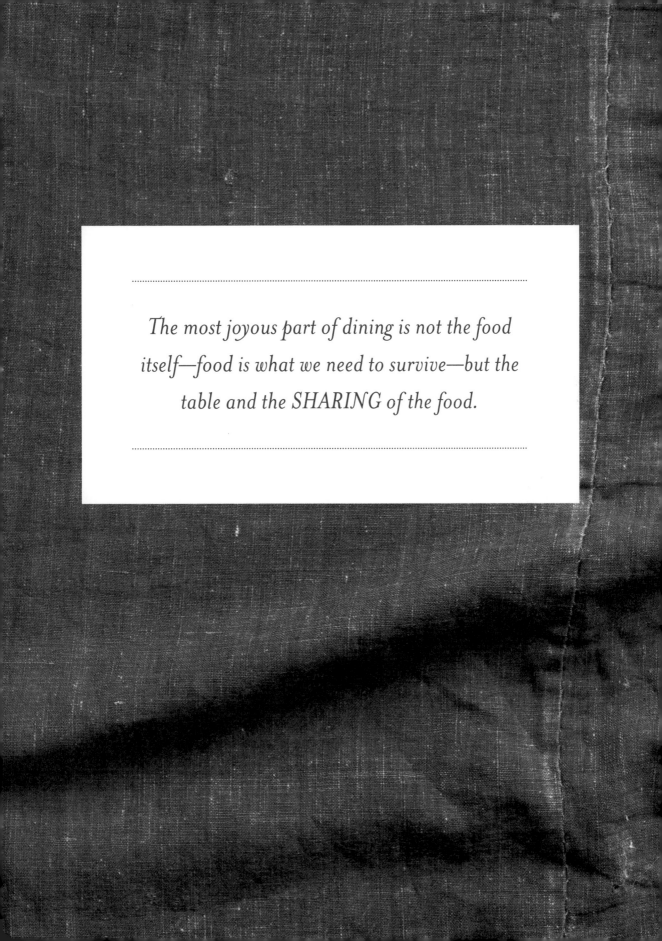

The most joyous part of dining is not the food itself—food is what we need to survive—but the table and the SHARING of the food.

SALADS ARE FOR CATERPILLARS

So where do we start? Simple, really. Let's look at this book's title: *Mr. Wilkinson's Well-Dressed Salads*. It's all in the name, they say. I can't tell you how many different thoughts have gone through my head in order to get to this title, but as time passed, it was the first title that sat well with me.

My first book, *Mr. Wilkinson's Vegetables*, was—like most things in life—about timing. It was my reflection, through recipes, of growing up, being in a kitchen and around food, and my philosophy (if we can use that word) about eating local and in-season food from a belief that these are the most flavorful and tastiest. It really is so simple: Buy the best tasty raw ingredients and foods from good producers, and the cook is already winning … then cook it properly and hey, you have delicious food! The same philosophy goes for this book—seasonal produce cooked well—but this time it's me looking at what I eat the most: salads!

So, why salads? Let me digress. I think of most food groups as a salad. Really I do. Why?

Well, the salad is one of the most diverse food groups ever in some way or form. A burger is a burger, and a curry is a curry … but salads are so wonderfully variable and can be hot or cold. Any ingredient can be made into a salad—any vegetable, fruit, grain, pulse, seafood or meat—not just salad leaves. A salad to me is simply a marriage of flavors and textures that you bring together, dress it with the right vinaigrette or dressing, and there you have it. For me, a salad primarily is designed to share, but on occasion, can be brilliant on its own for breakfast, lunch, or dinner, or any of the meals in between.

Which leads me to the question, do we all really think salads are just leaves or lettuce with other bits added? My little hooligan number 1, Finn Thomas, after asking him how he enjoyed the little pumpkin salad I made for our family dinner, replied, "No Dad, salad's for caterpillars!" This resonates so strongly with me—that we all think salads are simply just salad leaves. Which really is crazy! The category for salad leaves is just that, a category. I don't know any salad leaf called salad leaf. Arugula, witlof, mizuna, yes—but not salad leaf.

MY SALAD DAYS, AND A REVELATION

For those of you who don't know, I grew up in Barnsley, South Yorkshire, in that country called England. My father lived in a pub for some time, where my hospitality and culinary career really started. I worked for Rob Jane (my father's best mate Alan's son); he was my start-of-life mentor, who taught me to think for myself, work hard, and have fun while doing it.

The Crown & Cushion was the pub I grew up in, and was my first look at adult life and the meaning of work. The food on offer was very similar to most other pub food—the plate generally consisted of a form of meat or fish taking pride of place on the whole plate, some form of potato (generally French fries; we all love them) to cover the rest of the plate, and then you got asked by the wait staff, "Veggies or salad?" These really just being a plate filler.

It was this "salad" that offered my first insight as to what a "salad" was. We must have all seen it: Iceberg lettuce cup filled with slices of onion, cucumber, tomato, radish, grated carrot, and some baby mustard cress on top, served with a side of creamy dressing. It was the staple salad for the masses in pubs, clubs, and I guess any food place that served a main meal. This was my first thought of a salad—boring but refreshing, something "healthy" on the side of the meat and fries. When clearing tables in the pub, it fascinated me just how many people would leave the salad. "Not eating that rabbit food crap!" they would say. Back then, I would've had to agree.

My first insight into the workings of a professional kitchen was in Kingston upon Thames, on the outskirts of London, in a place called Warren House, under the guidance of mentor, friend, and head chef Michael Taylor. It was here at Warren House, in my first job as a chef at seventeen, that I really saw what a salad could be. There were dishes named Waldorf, Niçoise, Caesar, Caprese, Panzanella, and Cobb, all foreign to me back then; saying that, you couldn't get the old potato salad or coleslaw past me. In those two years of my life, I learned so much about cooking and being a chef, but the lunch salad section was my first real insight into a proper salad, how to make a dressing and the many different types, how to get the right ratio of dressing to the leaves or produce used, learning flavor combinations and textures that make for a better salad, and getting them all out on time.

However, it wasn't until I was the head chef of Circa in Melbourne, Australia, that I realized how good a salad could be, and how often I was making them and putting them on the menu, and not just as a side. Salad of this, or blah blah salad and so on … until I stopped to think how deeply entwined the salad is within all cuisines and cultures. It makes sense to me to make and eat a lot of salads, so if you have to define me as a chef, I guess I'm really good at doing seasonal salads, leaning on the vegetable side.

I really do think the concept of "salad" is changing in everybody's mind to be something other than just a leaf salad, and hopefully, the recipes that follow will help you think about salads a little differently too.

ABOUT THIS BOOK

I have divided the salads into four seasons, with a little introduction to each chapter as to what grows in each season and how I feel at that particular time of the year.

There are thirteen recipes per chapter as a guide to what to make during that season. Ideally I would love it if you made one salad a week, but see how you go. Please note that produce also often flows into the following season. Take tomatoes and basil, for example. These are a highlight of summer, but I was still picking stunning tomatoes in mid-autumn, and I made my last batch of pesto for the Mrs. and hooligans in late autumn.

At the end of each season is a dressings "family tree." Why? Well it annoys me that in many a cookbook there are some great recipes that can be used in so many other ways, but they don't tell you about it! I love Stephanie Alexander's *Cook's Companion* for this—how she notes what a certain item also goes well with—so I have included here, without recipes, a few other little things I would do with the dressings.

At the end of each season there is also a recipe for a fruit salad—simple fruits of the season that make for a delightful change to just a plain old fruit number. I love cordials, so I have also shared with you some different ones I make throughout the year, so you can capture the bounty of each season to enjoy at a later time.

A COUPLE OF TIPS TO FINISH

Sometimes it can feel like we're all starting to take cooking a little too seriously, making it a lot harder work than it should be. Whenever this happens, I close my eyes and think of my Nanna Rita pottering around the kitchen, not a stress in the world. If you do stress in the kitchen or at times don't enjoy the chore of cooking, try the following tips for size; it's what we do at home …

Cooking starts with organization, so what we do at the start of each week (although you could do this on any day that best suits you) is to simply write a list of what we are going to eat, or would like to eat, for the week. It brings us together, makes us talk—the old art of conversation!—but then we also know what to buy throughout the week. We are all generally busy, and there isn't anything worse than getting home, tired after work or from the kids, and figuring out what to bloody well cook.

And please, please, you don't have to cook every night. Go out, get some take-out—but if you do, just make it a good ethical choice.

Here is an example of what a week in the Wilkinson–Gibb Clan household sometimes looks like.

MEAL PLAN

MONDAY: Spaghetti bolognese

TUESDAY: Dinner at Pope Joan

WEDNESDAY: Free-range chicken schnitzel + zucchini salad (page 92)

THURSDAY: The Mrs' Silverbeet & Feta Pie (book 1) + egg salad (page 178)

FRIDAY: Takeaway meal from one of our favorite spots

SATURDAY: Vegetable & chickpea curry + brown rice salad (page 142)

SUNDAY: Corned beef with white sauce + carrots cooked in their own juice (page 215)

And lastly, please eat at the table and share food in the middle of the table. The most joyous part of dining is not the food itself—food is what we need to survive—but the table and the *sharing* of the food. To keep in contact and gather information, to spend some time with family or friends, to talk, laugh, and even cry—the table is where we get the chance to stop, catch up with our loved ones, then enjoy the food. The food is a tool: The more delicious it is, the easier it is to talk about it, but it's just a tool in our life to talk to one another and enjoy each other's company.

I truly hope you enjoy *Mr. Wilkinson's Well-Dressed Salads* … and, like me, start to think of the salad as a truly unique and wonderful thing.

GROWING & USING SALAD LEAVES

Now that I've explained what a salad is to me, it would seem weird not to tell you a little bit of the history of the salad, give a little guide on how I grow salad leaves, and offer some basic salad dressings that go with different leaves and other tasty things.

MY POTTED HISTORY OF THE SALAD

There is surely a little history out there stating where the salad originated, but I will tell you my version and if I'm wrong, well, never mind.

Documentation tells us that the Egyptians and Greeks all had a version of salad, but I'm going to stick with the Romans—they did build great roads after all. Salad derives from the word "salt," and it was believed Romans used to salt their vegetables and take them on their voyages of discovery, later rinsing off the salt and adding what are now known as edible weeds—basically, they foraged for green leaves to add to their veggies. These leaves were believed to be anything in the cabbage, knotweed, goosefoot, grass, legume, amaranth, and sunflower families, and many of these are what we use as salad leaves today.

In more recent times, and still in common practice today in many parts of the world, the salad is seen as a cleanser of sorts, taken after a meal to freshen the palate and help the digestive system relax a little before the next course—or, as seen on many a menu, it is enjoyed at the start of a meal as an appetizer.

In many a household or restaurant, the salad has become a name for a side or something to accompany your main meal—or the salad part is put at the end or beginning of a dish, when basically the chef hasn't got a clue what to call the little devil of a dish. No matter where it came from, the salad is thankfully with us.

THE LEAVES OF THE SALAD

So I'm at the back door step—it truly doesn't matter what season it is—bowl and scissors in hand, off to snip me some leaves.

We really do take salad leaves for granted. Just think, we all generally just grab a head of lettuce or bag some leaves from the supermarket or greengrocer, not really thinking about their taste—the most important factor in the food we prepare—or their texture. These are the two main features of a salad leaf.

Salad-leaf growing has changed a lot in the past decade or two, just as all of agriculture has changed, really—trying to grow for the mass population so we can have what we want, when we want it.

But take a minute, please … if we have the ability, or more importantly the space, I think we all should grow salad leaves and herbs in our garden, balcony, or yes, even our windowsills. The salad leaves we now see on the supermarket shelves are more often than not grown hydroponically, with quick production as the foremost principle, with little thought to its flavor and texture.

We've all done it: bought some leaves, placed them in our "crisper" in the fridge, then come back to them at a later stage, only to throw the limp leaves away.

When making a leaf salad, its freshness is surely more important than with any other vegetable or fruit we grow. Most other fresh produce can survive a bit but, in my opinion, not the salad leaf.

Here is something else to ponder: A single head of romaine lettuce (cos) costs substantially more than a tray of seedlings. A packet of seeds costs a few dollars at most and yields about 30–40 lettuces. I'm okay at math, and that adds up nicely to me (I am originally from Yorkshire, you know!). So basically I'm saying, grow your own …

GROW, YOU GOOD THINGS …

So how to grow these little beauties? Well, all my information here is just a guide. If you really want to learn more, there are many great books out there, or just head down to your local nursery and chat with the staff—they are full of information (more correct than I) appropriate for the season and climate you are in. I always leave a nursery thinking, "Damn, I should have known that!"

Lettuces can generally be grown all year round, except in the really hot months. A few years back, I bit into a butter lettuce—my favorite of all lettuces—in the height of summer, and it was bitter as all buggery. It was simply trying to keep its very being alive by going to seed, of course. The structure and taste of all plants change once they go to seed or are in the process of bolting and about to go to seed.

My rule of thumb for growing **lettuces** through summer and into early autumn is to pick a nice shaded area, which gets a little sun for a part of the day (ideally the first sun or late sun). If the lettuces are in full sun, they will more likely bolt and become bitter … but one way around this is to cover them with a shade cloth. In late autumn through spring, grow your lettuces in a nice sunny spot. And yes, they do grow in winter in cooler to mild climates, but not in areas where hard frost and snow occur, unless you have them covered (in a green house, for instance).

As a rule, for the "**mustard leaves**," "**soft leaves**," and "**herbs**," I sow seeds directly into the ground. I keep them well watered until I see their heads pop up (roughly 4–10 days), then lightly water them every day or so, depending on the season—more in summer. Make sure you don't directly water the leaves; in the past I have "burned" leaves by doing this, as they are fragile. I usually thin them (i.e. remove the excess seedlings, allowing the others to grow) at about 14 days, then most should be ready to harvest in another 14–40 days. Not bad, hey! Obviously, the timing will depend on the particular climate you are in.

For the "**hearty & crunchy**" and "**bitter leaves**," I like to prepare a seed tray or an old polystyrene box filled with good seed-raising mix, which I keep watered until the seeds sprout. Then I generally transplant to the garden at 14–20 days, or until they look big enough to cope. Keep them tightly planted, I say—it gives them enough room to grow, but also keeps them from flopping over too far, and I like a smaller lettuce. When harvesting these, I like to take the outside leaves off rather than cutting off the whole head—and as a general rule I quickly run out the back and collect the leaves just before serving the meal, give them a quick wash under cold water, spin or dry lightly in a towel, then add my dressing and serve.

SALAD FRIENDS AND FOES

There are a few good tips when growing salad leaves. I like to put them in with marigolds, as these are a great companion plant—as are radishes, carrots, and onions. And my arugula (rocket) goes gangbusters near strawberries.

Remember slugs and snails love salad leaves. Scattering a few used coffee grounds around will help stop them, or go out late at night with a torch and collect them in a container, then place them on your bird feeder or on the lawn for the birds to enjoy the next morning.

In my head, I group salad leaves into the following categories; this is simply my thought process into them, rather than conventional wisdom. I've also given some examples as to what kind of leaves are in each category. My perfect salad would be a mixture of one or two or all of them.

I also love herbs in a leaf salad, especially mint, sorrel, and tarragon. They add such a delicate and interesting layer to the flavor.

HEARTY & CRUNCHY

- Romaine (cos) lettuce
- Boston (little gem) lettuce
- Speckled romaine (cos) lettuce
- Iceberg lettuce
- Butter lettuce (a favorite of mine)
- Mignonette lettuce (the bronze and green varieties)

BITTER LEAVES

- Witlof (Belgian endive/chicory)
- Radicchio (little Italian markets often sell a range of interesting radicchio seeds)
- Belgian endive
- Dandelions (which I always thought were best for rabbits!)

MUSTARD LEAVES

- Nasturtium leaves
- Watercress
- Upland cress
- Arugula (rocket)
- Baby green and red mustard leaves

SOFT LEAVES

- Lollo bianco and rosso lettuce
- Green and red oak leaf lettuce
- Baby spinach leaves
- Mâche (lamb's lettuce/corn salad)
- Mizuna
- Purslane
- Salad bowl lettuce (red and green varieties)

SALAD HERBS

- Parsley
- Mint (I love its freshness in a salad!)
- Chives
- Basil
- Tarragon
- Sorrel

OTHER

- Fava bean (broad bean) tops
- Pea tendrils
- Micro shoots, such as radish, beet, alfalfa, fenugreek, and kale

*It really is so simple: Buy the best tasty raw
ingredients and foods from good producers,
and the cook is already winning …*

MY ESSENTIAL DRESSINGS

It's funny how many salads I have eaten where the ratio of dressing to salad ingredients is all wrong.

This is the fundamental trick to getting the perfect harmony and balance in the salad as a dish. Too much dressing and your salad is sodden; too little and it can be dry and plain.

Less is sometimes more, so dress gently. You wouldn't go out wearing hat, scarf, and coat in summer, now would you, or shorts and tank top in winter … It's about simply dressing an item well, whether it's you or your food!

A dressing is not always essential either. Many times I just add a simple splash of beautiful extra-virgin olive oil or great quality vinegar, whether it's cherry, balsamic, or apple cider vinegar. Sometimes it's a tablespoon of yogurt or some crushed berries such as blueberries or raspberries.

Also don't forget about any cooking juices from the tray or pan you might've cooked one of the ingredients in. Add a dash of something acidic (lemon juice or vinegar), check the seasoning, then kapow, you have a new dressing!

That said, these next recipes are the go-to dressings I use at Pope Joan and at home.

SIMPLE LEMON

This is a salad dressing basic we have on hand for so many dishes.

Makes about 1½ cups (375 ml, 13 fl oz)

¼ cup (60 ml, 2 fl oz) lemon juice (juice of 2–3 lemons)
1 teaspoon dijon mustard
1 teaspoon superfine (caster) sugar
1 teaspoon sea salt
1 cup (250 ml, 8 fl oz) sunflower oil or canola oil (non-GMO)
¼ cup (50 ml, 2 fl oz) hot water

In a bowl, whisk together the lemon juice, mustard, sugar, and salt. Slowly whisk in the oil until fully incorporated, then whisk in the water. The dressing will keep for 6 weeks in an airtight jar in the fridge.

USES: A good all-rounder for all types of salad leaves, and great for salads containing radish or fruit. Also nice with smoked fish or crabmeat.

A FRENCHMAN'S MAYO

This is from an old friend of mine, a chef called Manu from my time at Warren House. It is my base mayo for all sorts of things. **Makes about 1¼ cups (340 ml, 11 oz)**

2 egg yolks

2 teaspoons dijon mustard

1½ cups (375 ml, 13 fl oz) sunflower oil or mild flavored vegetable oil

2 tablespoons (20 ml, 1 fl oz) good quality white wine vinegar

sea salt to taste

In a bowl, whisk together the egg yolks and mustard until the yolks turn pale. Slowly whisk in the oil until fully combined, then add the vinegar and season to your liking—I prefer to just add sea salt.

The mayo will keep for 1 week in an airtight jar in the fridge.

USES: Well, what would a potato salad be without mayo?

SALAD CREAM

A Frenchman's mayo, given a bit of English. Let's be honest, salad cream kicks the bejeebers out of the Frenchies' mayo. What would the English do without it? **Makes about 2 cups (500 ml, 17 fl oz)**

1 tablespoon superfine (caster) sugar

½ cup (100 ml, 4 fl oz) hot water

2 egg yolks

2 teaspoons dijon mustard

1½ cups (375 ml, 13 fl oz) sunflower oil or mild flavored vegetable oil

3 tablespoons (40 ml, 1½ fl oz) good quality white wine vinegar

½ cup (100 ml, 4 fl oz) light (pouring, single) cream

sea salt to taste

Dissolve the sugar in the hot water. In a bowl, whisk together the egg yolks and mustard until the yolks turn pale, then slowly whisk in the oil until fully combined. Now whisk in the vinegar, cream, and the hot water, then season to your liking. Again, I prefer to just add sea salt.

The salad cream will keep for 1 week in an airtight jar in the fridge.

USES: No salad sandwich is the same without salad cream. Also use it with any "hearty & crunchy" salad leaf.

ENGLISH MUSTARD CREAM

I love this dressing. It's a staple dressing in my world—a quick, easy one for all sorts of dishes.
Makes about 1¼ cups (350 ml, 11 fl oz)

¼ cup (60 g, 2 oz) hot English mustard

¼ cup (50 ml, 2 fl oz) chardonnay vinegar

1 cup (250 ml, 8 fl oz) light (pouring, single) cream

2 pinches of sea salt

2 pinches of sugar

In a bowl, whisk everything together. The dressing will keep for 2 months in an airtight jar in the fridge.

USES: Another "hearty & crunchy" salad leaf dressing, but also great with steamed potato salad, raw cauliflower salad, and green beans. You can add chopped anchovies for a cheat's Caesar salad, but don't tell anyone I said that …

CLASSIC BUT A LITTLE POSH

Similar to an Italian dressing, this is a vinegar and oil-based dressing from my time at Martin Wishart's in Scotland. It keeps well in the fridge. **Makes about 1 cup (250 ml, 8 fl oz)**

½ cup (100 ml, 4 fl oz) extra-virgin olive oil

⅓ cup (80 ml, 2½ fl oz) walnut oil

2 tablespoons (30 ml, 1½ fl oz) good quality red wine vinegar

1 small shallot, finely chopped

1 garlic clove, finely chopped

1 teaspoon sea salt

6 tarragon leaves

In a bowl, whisk together the olive oil, walnut oil, and vinegar. In another bowl, mix together the shallot, garlic, salt, and tarragon leaves. Let sit for a few minutes to infuse, then stir into the oil mixture.

The dressing will keep in a jar in the fridge for months, but remember to bring it back to room temperature a good 20 minutes before using.

USES: Generally, I keep this dressing away from the "hearty & crunchy" salad leaves, but it's fine if you're using a mixture of all leaf varieties. This is my favorite on the bitter, mustard, and soft leaves. It's also great with roasted vegetable salads and grains.

BASICS

DUKKAH

I add a little sugar to my dukkah, as I think it helps bring out the flavor of all the other spices. It's a great way to add taste and texture to dishes, and I love it. **Makes about 1 cup (225 g)**

INGREDIENTS

⅔ cup (100 g, 3½ oz) hazelnuts

2 teaspoons white peppercorns

1 tablespoon coriander seeds

1 tablespoon sesame seeds

2 teaspoons ground cumin seeds

1½ tablespoons salt

1 tablespoon soft brown sugar

METHOD

Preheat the oven to 350ºF (180ºC, Gas 4). Put the hazelnuts on a baking tray and roast for 5–10 minutes. While they're still warm, place them in a tea towel (dish towel) and rub off the skins. Set aside.

Put a flat-bottomed frying pan over low heat. Add the peppercorns and coriander seeds and allow to toast gently, shaking the pan all the time, until you see some smoke or steam rising from the spices. Quickly tip them into a bowl to cool them, so they don't get a chance to burn.

Now lightly toast the sesame seeds and cumin seeds separately, shaking the pan constantly, and tipping them into separate bowls.

Using a mortar and pestle, grind the hazelnuts to break them up. Add the peppercorn mixture and grind to a milled pepper consistency. Now add the toasted sesame seeds, cumin seeds, salt, and sugar, mixing well.

The dukkah will keep in an airtight container in a cool dark spot for several months.

PICKLED SHALLOTS

I find myself using a lot of pickles, and why not ... Their acidity brings new life to so many dishes and also helps clean the palate up a little. **Makes about 1 cup (225 g)**

INGREDIENTS

⅓ cup (80 ml, 2½ fl oz) rice wine vinegar

⅓ cup (80 ml, 2½ fl oz) apple cider vinegar

½ cup (150 g, 5½ oz) superfine (caster) sugar

1 teaspoon fine salt

4 shallots, thinly sliced into rings, then separated

METHOD

Put the vinegars, sugar, and salt in a saucepan with ⅔ cup (150 ml, 5 fl oz) water. Bring to a boil, then take off the heat. Cool to room temperature, then chill.

Place the shallot rings in a container and pour the pickling liquid over. Leave to pickle for 30 minutes and the shallots are ready to use. They are best enjoyed fresh, but will keep for a few days in the fridge.

CHEAT'S TIP: Adding a nip of grenadine to the pickling liquid will dye the shallots an amazing pink color.

ROMESCO SAUCE

Romesco is brilliant as a dip or sauce for any vegetable, meat, or fish. Keep this one in the fridge (it will keep for ages), so you have a delicious sauce on hand at all times. **Makes about 3 cups (750 ml, 25½ fl oz)**

INGREDIENTS

5 red bell peppers (capsicums), (about 850 g, 1 lb 13 oz)

⅓ cup (75 ml, 2½ fl oz) olive oil

2 oregano sprigs

2 thyme sprigs

⅓ cup (85 g, 3 oz) quince paste

⅓ cup (50 g, 1¾ oz) blanched almonds, chopped

1 garlic clove

pinch of fennel seeds

pinch of coriander seeds

pinch of chamushka (nigella) seeds (see glossary)

pinch of cumin seeds

pinch of ground sumac (see glossary)

1–2 teaspoons salt

¾ cup (180 ml, 6 fl oz) extra-virgin olive oil

2 tablespoons (20 ml, 1 fl oz) cabernet vinegar or red wine vinegar

METHOD

Preheat the oven to 425ºF (220ºC, Gas 7). Place the peppers in a roasting pan and drizzle with the olive oil. Add the oregano and thyme sprigs and mix together. Roast for 40–50 minutes, shaking the pan every 8 minutes or so, until the peppers are soft and the skins nicely browned.

Take them out of the oven, cover with foil, and let the peppers steam for 10 minutes so they'll be easy to peel.

Carefully peel the peppers, and remove all the seeds. Place the flesh in a food processor, along with the quince paste, almonds, and garlic. Blitz to a purée. Add the spices, salt to taste, and blitz again.

Pour into a bowl, then fold in the extra-virgin olive oil and vinegar. Now check for a nice salt and acid balance, and you're done.

The sauce will keep well in an airtight container in the fridge for up to 1 week.

NOTE: See the salad dressing family tree on page 232 for other wicked ways to serve up your Romesco Sauce.

TOMATO KASUNDI

I love this relish so much I brought it out in retail. It is always in my fridge, both at home and at work. It's also a terrific base for a cheat's curry if you're in a hurry. **Makes enough to fill two 4-cup (1 liter, 34 fl oz) jars**

INGREDIENTS

4½ oz (125 g) knob of fresh ginger, peeled and chopped

⅓ cup (70 g, 2½ oz) peeled garlic

¾ oz (20 g) green chilies, cut in half and seeded

¾ cup plus 2 tablespoons (200 ml, 7 fl oz) canola oil (non-GMO)

1 tablespoon ground turmeric

½ cup (50 g, 2 oz) ground cumin

1 teaspoon chili powder

2 lb 10 oz (1.2 kg) canned chopped tomatoes

3 tablespoons (40 g, 1½ oz) fine sea salt

1¼ cups (340 ml, 11 fl oz) apple cider vinegar

½ cup (150 g, 5½ oz) unrefined soft brown sugar

METHOD

Chop the ginger, garlic, and chilli in a food processor until a smooth paste forms. Set aside.

Warm the canola oil in a heavy-bottomed 12-cup (3 liter, 101 fl oz) capacity saucepan over medium heat. Add the turmeric, cumin, and chilli powder and gently toast for 5 minutes to release the natural oils. Stir in the ginger mixture and cook for another 5 minutes.

Add the tomatoes, salt, vinegar, and sugar. Bring to a boil, then reduce the heat and simmer for 1–1½ hours. When the oil has risen to the top and the mixture looks like a curry, the pickle is ready.

Take off the heat; pour into sterilized jam jars and seal. The kasundi will keep in a cool dark place for at least a year. Once opened, store in the fridge and use within 3 months.

SOUTH PARK TOWNSHIP LIBRARY

SMOKED TOMATOES

A recipe from my first book, made by David Sr. and David Jr. from The Melbourne Pantry. I love these guys nearly as much as I love their smoked tomatoes. **Makes as much as you need**

INGREDIENTS

ripe roma (plum) tomatoes, white central cores cut out

superfine (caster) sugar, for sprinkling

salt to taste

freshly ground black pepper

a good handful of woodchips suitable for smoking

METHOD

To smoke the tomatoes, you'll need an 8-cup (2 liter, 68 fl oz) pot, a bowl filled with icy cold water, a roasting pan large enough to hold your tomatoes (but small enough to still fit in your fridge), a wire rack that will fit inside your roasting pan, and a spare shelf in your fridge.

Fill your pot with 4 cups (1 liter, 24 fl oz) of water and bring to a boil over high heat. Lower your tomatoes into the water, being careful of hot splashes, and leave for 10 seconds. Scoop out with a slotted spoon and submerge the tomatoes in iced water to blanch them.

Now peel the tomatoes, then rub each one with sugar, salt, and freshly ground black pepper. Place them on the wire rack.

Heat the smoking chips in a wok or frying pan. When they start to smoke, tip them into your roasting pan, then sit the rack of tomatoes on top. Cover with foil, pierce five holes in the foil, then it's into the oven for 5 minutes. Take out right away.

Place the roasting pan in the fridge on a thick tea towel (dish towel) so your fridge shelves don't melt. Leave until the tomatoes are cool.

So now you have smoked tomatoes! They will keep in an airtight container in the fridge for about 7 days.

SMOKED YOGURT

A recipe made for me by the cheeky chaps from The Melbourne Pantry. It came about after (my now partner) Sharlee asked if I knew someone who could smoke butter for a top British chef who was appearing at the Melbourne Food & Wine Festival. It made me think, how would smoking yogurt be, and ... well, it rocks. **Makes about 1 cup (250 g, 8 oz)**

INGREDIENTS

1 cup (250 g, 8 oz) Greek-style yogurt

1 handful woodchips suitable for smoking; I like apple or hickory chips

METHOD

Line a cast-iron wok with a double layer of foil. Scatter the woodchips in the middle, then place a wire rack on top.

Put the yogurt in a small metal bowl, then set it on top of a slightly larger bowl that has ice in it. (This will prevent the yogurt curdling during smoking.)

Place the wok over a high heat and get the woodchips smoking. Set the ice bowl (containing the bowl of yogurt) on the rack. Place a tight-fitting lid on top — or you could also use a large bowl turned upside down as a lid.

Smoke over high heat for 5 minutes. Turn off the heat, remove the lid, and carefully remove the yogurt bowl.

Whisk the yogurt back together, transfer to a fresh bowl, then cover and refrigerate until required. The smoked yogurt will keep for 7–10 days in the fridge.

NOTE: It can be good to do this outside using a small portable gas cooker, as it gets pretty smoky inside!

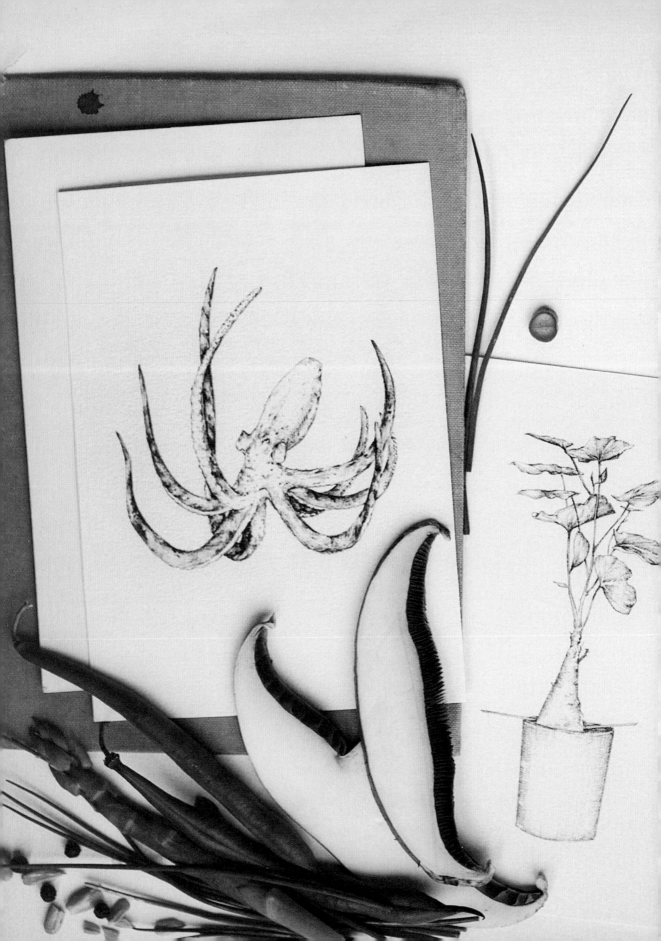

SPRING

SPRING

BEFORE I TALK ABOUT SPRING SPECIFICALLY, I WANT TO TALK ABOUT THE SEASONS IN GENERAL. BECAUSE THE THING ABOUT SEASONS IS THAT THEY ARE REALLY FLUID—THEY'RE NOT CUT-AND-DRIED.

Plants bud and bloom, depending on the sun and the rain, and the seasons aren't really the three months that we humans have tried to arrange them into. They roll into one another. It isn't necessarily scorching on the first day of summer, just as it isn't guaranteed to be frosty on the first day of winter. You can feel the changes coming in the weeks leading up to the end of one season and the beginning of the next, and the way the plants and animals behave also give us clues as to what is coming.

Our calendar means nothing to good old Mother Nature—she just throws the seasons at us. Australia's Indigenous people, with their innate connection to the land, actually believe there are six seasons that influence the birds, animals, and, of course, plant life. The indicators of seasonal change are all taken from when plants bud and bloom, when certain reptiles hibernate, when animals birth their young, and even when birds moult their feathers. The Indigenous seasons are highly respectful to the land, and I really think that we forget in the rush of our modern lives that respect for the environment is so important. We need to take care of Mother Nature because she takes care of us.

But let's talk about spring. Springtime is all about renewal. It's right there in the name, isn't it? Everything 'springs' back to life after the dormancy of winter. The bulbs are starting to come through, and green shoots poke their heads out of the ground. There is new life all around, from animals and their young to the grass starting to wake up with the warmth of the sun after winter's chill has passed. Creatures are emerging from hibernation—hedgehogs in Britain, and in Australia yabbies and eels are coming out of their burrows. Spring makes me think of mowing the lawn in shirtsleeves when I was back in the United Kingdom and the smell of onion weed as the mower ran over it. No other smell makes me think so much of spring.

The daffodils and tulips bloom and give us back some of the color we have missed. Winter is either incredibly green or bare. In spring the color comes back, like a sneak preview of summer. Here in Australia, it conjures images of gorgeous flowering wattle, all bright greens and gold. The wattle is so vibrant it's easy to see why this combination has been adopted as the national colors.

There is an innate sense of hopefulness about spring. It's easy to become a bit low and depressed by the bleakness of winter, especially if there is a lot of rain, but spring acts as a restorative. Everything is warming up and shaking off the frostiness of winter.

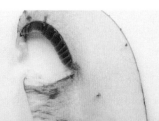

No wonder there are festivals all around the world dedicated to spring's arrival. Many countries boast a tradition of celebrating the spring equinox. There are actually two equinoxes every year—one in spring and one in autumn. An equinox is a day in the solar calendar that is marked by the day and night being of equal length. The spring (or vernal) equinox was considered of particular spiritual significance to many cultures, and entwined with the notion of resurrection and rebirth—not only in the Christian calendar but also within age-old Egyptian and Mayan beliefs. There is evidence that the ancient Cambodian temple at Angkor Wat is aligned to the spring equinox. For many cultures, the equinox represents the struggle between the forces of good and evil—of the light versus the dark.

In the garden you start to see some of the berries and tropical fruits shooting and getting ready for their peak in summer. Rhubarb, mandarins, and oranges are all in their prime, from their kick-off in winter.

We all think of spring lamb and spring as symbols of verdant fertility, but we can even see the effects of seasonality in produce we don't usually think of—such as milk, for example. Like every other living thing, the quality of the feed in the paddock is affected by the seasons and the amount of sun and rain. Spring is the pinnacle of good pasture for farmers, after the paddocks have woken up from their winter dormancy, when the ground has thawed and softened. There is (hopefully) plenty of rain, and the sun is warm and gentle. The searing heat of summer is still some months away.

If you follow this principle along the food chain, it then affects other things like the quality of milk that is coming from animals, and then the quality of produce that is made with that milk—you may not realize that even cheese comes into season! For my good friends Ann-Marie and Carla at Holy Goat farm in Victoria, spring is when their farm really kicks into action. The goats kid in spring, which increases milk yield, but the quality of the milk is also improved by the amount and variety of fodder that is available to the goats in the fields. All this combines to produce peak cheese-making season. And the cheeses themselves change according to all the variables in the actual milk, such as the taste, aroma, color, and fat content. Do yourself a favor and try some gorgeous fresh goat's cheese in spring.

And when it comes to the ultimate in spring vegetables? I've said it before in my first book, but I'm going to say it again, just so you know I really mean it. If there is one vegetable that you should wait for spring to enjoy, please make it asparagus. Just like cherries in summer, the season is short but plentiful. Asparagus is just so crisp and delicious when it is young and fresh, and the price drops so dramatically that you can have it at every meal, if you want.

And why wouldn't you want to?

SESAME-FRIED ASPARAGUS WITH SASHIMI & MISO

This is just one of many beautiful dishes Vanessa Mateus, my nighttime head chef at Pope Joan, has created. The textures and flavors are just divine. We love using asparagus, and I have to thank Trevor and Jo Courtney from Bridge Farm organics for supplying our stunning asparagus for many, many years now. **Serves 2**

INGREDIENTS

8 asparagus spears, woody ends trimmed, then cut in half

⅓ cup (50 g, 1¾ oz) all-purpose (plain) flour

1 free-range egg, beaten

⅔ cup (100 g, 3½ oz) sesame seeds

¼ cup (50 ml, 2 fl oz) apple cider vinegar

3 tablespoons (50 g, 1¾ oz) sugar

2 champion radishes (round ones), thinly sliced

3 tablespoons (50 g, 1¾ oz) mayonnaise

2 teaspoons (10 g, ¼ oz) red miso paste

4 cups (1 liter, 34 fl oz) canola oil (non-GMO)

7 oz (200 g) sashimi-style white fish fillets, such as halibut or snapper, pin-boned and thinly sliced

juice of 1 lime

salt to taste

olive oil, for drizzling

METHOD

Bring a pot of water to a boil; add the asparagus and cook for 30 seconds. Take out and refresh under cold water. Once cold, pat the asparagus with paper towels until dry.

Dip each asparagus spear into the flour, then the beaten egg, allowing any excess egg to drip off, then into the sesame seeds. Set aside.

In a small pot, bring the vinegar, sugar, and ¼ cup (50 ml, 1¾ fl oz) water to a boil, then take off the heat and set aside to cool. Once cool, add the radish.

In a small bowl, mix together the mayonnaise and miso.

Pour the canola oil into a saucepan, ensuring the pan is no more than one-third full. Heat to 325°F (170°C) on a cooking thermometer, then deep-fry the asparagus in two batches for 3–4 minutes each time, or until light golden. Remove each batch with a slotted spoon and drain on paper towels.

Dollop the miso mayo onto a serving plate. Slice the asparagus spears and arrange on the plate, then lay the fish slices around. Sprinkle the lime juice over the fish and season with salt. Now drain the pickled radish and arrange over the top. Finish by drizzling with a little olive oil.

NOTE: The sesame-fried asparagus is great on its own as a canapé; you could also serve it by itself in a bowl with the miso mayo as a dipping sauce.

SALAD OF GLOBE ARTICHOKES, CARROTS, BEANS & PICKLED RADISH

I truly love this dish. There's a bit of work in preparing and cooking the old globe artichoke, so if you think it's too hard and puts you off making this salad, go out and buy yourself a small jar of preserved baby artichokes instead—I would if I was cooking at home. This salad is also lovely with a simple grilled fish like mullet or albacore tuna. **Serves 4**

INGREDIENTS

2 tablespoons (20 ml, 1 fl oz) apple cider vinegar

1 tablespoon salt

6 globe artichokes

8 baby carrots, washed well and sliced into rounds about ¼ in (5 mm) thick

2 oz (60 g) green beans, thinly sliced

1 tablespoon blonde sultanas (golden raisins)

olive oil, for drizzling

½ teaspoon ground sumac (see glossary), plus extra for sprinkling

pinch of ras el hanout (see glossary)

salt to taste

freshly ground black pepper

1 small handful flat-leaf (Italian) parsley, washed and roughly chopped

½ cup (100 g, 3½ oz) Greek-style yogurt

PICKLED RADISH

½ cup (100 ml, 4 fl oz) rice wine vinegar, or any white vinegar

3 tablespoons (50 g, 1¾ oz) superfine (caster) sugar

2 shallots, thinly sliced

4 radishes, trimmed and cut into quarters

METHOD

Pour 8 cups (2 liters, 68 fl oz) water into a large pot. Add the apple cider vinegar and salt and set aside.

To prepare the artichokes, first peel off the outer hard layers of leaves. Trim the stalks about 1¼ inches (3 cm) from the base. Cut 1½ inches (4 cm) off the pointy top bit. Peel the stalk part, then cut the artichokes into quarters lengthways. Using a teaspoon, scrape out the fluffy bits in the middle, then add the artichokes to the pot.

Bring the pot to a boil, reduce the heat, and simmer with a lid on for 6 minutes. Add the carrots and cook for a further 4–5 minutes, or until the artichokes are done; they are cooked when you can insert a small sharp knife through with ease.

Add the beans and cook for a further 1 minute. Take off the stove and let sit for 5 minutes. Strain, discarding the liquid, then place the veggie mixture in a bowl. Add the sultanas, then cover.

Meanwhile, prepare the pickled radish. In a small pot, bring the rice vinegar, sugar, and 3 tablespoons (40 ml, 1¾ fl oz) water to the boil. Take off the heat and let the liquid cool for 5 minutes. Put the shallot and radish in a heatproof bowl, pour the pickling liquid over, and let sit for 5 minutes. Drain the pickle mixture and add to the bowl with the artichokes.

Add a splash of olive oil to the veggies, along with the sumac, ras el hanout, and some salt and freshly ground black pepper. Toss in the parsley, then arrange on a platter. Dollop the yogurt around the dish, sprinkle with a little extra sumac, add a final drizzle of olive oil, and then it's ready to eat.

EARLY SPRING

There is something annoying yet so wonderful about early spring in the garden. It has sat on the fence, not too sure if the cold air at night means more chill is to come, or heed the delightful midday sun saying that warmer weather is on its way. The garden itself is trying so hard, and weeds are everywhere, which reminds me that I have neglected her for a while, like you neglect your dog when your first-born child arrives.

I'm eager to get into the garden to plant, but still not too sure about what and when. My crop of fava (broad) beans has flowered and small buds are appearing; the celery is so good I have to eat it there and then. My farmer friends are delighted by the first signs of asparagus, and tell me the avocados are looking amazing, but many are worried, hoping there won't be a late frost that could end their season of growing just as it has begun.

RECIPE:

GREEN HERB, CELERY & FAVA BEAN TOPS

A perfect quick salad for me is to head out and snip some tops off the fava (broad) beans, harvest some of the smaller celery stalks, using the leaves and thinly slicing the stalks, then mixing these with some torn parsley, the shoots of some sorrel, and leaves of mint. Simply dress these with a dash of red wine vinegar, a little sea salt, and a drizzle of hazelnut oil. Maybe toss through some soft goat's feta and serve.

SALAD OF TOFU, SNAKE BEANS & CRISPY SHALLOT WITH BLACK BEAN VINAIGRETTE

The black bean vinaigrette is a version from my old mate Jake Nicolson, and has become a regular at home and in dishes for work. This dish goes brilliantly with some simple Chinese-style roasted beef, duck, or chicken. **Serves 2, or 4 sharing**

INGREDIENTS

14 oz (400 g) Chinese yard-long (snake) beans

10½ oz (300 g) organic silken tofu, cut into 8 pieces

1 small handful cilantro (coriander), leaves picked and washed

1 tablespoon crispy fried Asian shallots (from a jar)

BLACK BEAN VINAIGRETTE

7 tablespoons (100 g, 3½ oz) fermented black beans (see glossary), soaked overnight in the fridge in several changes of water (or you can use 3 tablespoons black bean paste, from a jar)

1 small long red chili, seeded and finely chopped

3 shallots, finely diced

1¾ oz (50 g) knob of fresh ginger, peeled and finely grated

1¼ cups (340 ml, 11 fl oz) canola oil (non-GMO)

⅔ cup (150 ml, 5 fl oz) light soy sauce

3 tablespoons (40 ml, 1½ fl oz) black rice vinegar, or rice vinegar

METHOD

To make the vinaigrette, rinse the soaked black beans if you're using fermented ones. Place in a bowl and use a fork to smash them up a little, to a paste-like consistency. Add the chili, shallots, and ginger, then carefully fold in the canola oil, soy sauce, and vinegar. Taste for a nice salt and acid balance and adjust to your liking.

Bring a large pot of water to a boil. Cut the snake beans into thirds, then add to the pot and boil for 3 minutes, or until they're still a little crisp but cooked.

Drain the hot beans and place in a mixing bowl. Add half the tofu and cilantro, and enough dressing to coat (roughly 3 tablespoons). Gently toss, not breaking up the tofu too much, then place in a serving dish.

Add the remaining tofu. Dress with a little more vinaigrette and the rest of the cilantro. Serve sprinkled with the fried shallots.

NOTE: See the salad dressing family tree on page 80 for other great uses for the Black Bean Vinaigrette. Any leftover vinaigrette will keep in an airtight jar in the fridge for weeks.

There is new life all around, from animals and their young to the grass starting to wake up with the warmth of the sun after winter's chill has passed. Creatures are emerging from hibernation—woodchucks in America, hedgehogs in Britain, and in Australia yabbies and eels are coming out of their burrows.

RADISHES & CHILI

A really simple salad or snack. We list this one in the snacks section of the menu at Pope Joan. Seriously, radishes never tasted so good. You can leave out the biltong, as the dish is just as good without it, but I love it in. **Serves 2, or 4 as a little snack**

INGREDIENTS

20 sparkler, champion, or cherry belle radishes, trimmed

1 tablespoon fine salt

1 cup (250 ml, 8 fl oz) canola oil (non-GMO)

2 tablespoons (20 ml, 1 fl oz) sesame oil

¼ cup (50 ml, 2 fl oz) soy sauce

2 tablespoons (20 ml, 1 fl oz) black rice vinegar

1 tablespoon superfine (caster) sugar

1 long red chili, halved

1 teaspoon chili flakes

2 ounces (50 g) biltong, beef jerky, or prosciutto, thinly sliced (optional)

1 tablespoon chopped flat-leaf (Italian) parsley

METHOD

Crack each radish by hitting it with the bottom of a pot or a mallet. You don't want to completely crack or split them — just crush or break the skins in parts. Once they're all done, place them into a bowl, add the salt and thoroughly mix through. Let them sit for 20 minutes, then rinse under cold water to wash off most of the salt. Dry.

Place the canola oil, sesame oil, soy sauce, vinegar, sugar, chili, and chili flakes in a large pot and bring to a boil. Once boiling, add the radishes, then bring back to a boil. Immediately take off the heat and let sit for 5 minutes.

Take the warm radishes out of the pot and place in a bowl. Add the biltong, if using, and parsley; toss together and serve.

SALAD OF SALT COD, FRISÉE & CROUTONS WITH BACON VINAIGRETTE

You really should read Mark Kurlansky's books on the subjects of both salt and cod—brilliantly written and so interesting. That said, there are different quality versions of salt cod. For this dish please grab the expensive whole salted fillet; generally you can get them boned. Bear in mind you will need to soak the salt cod for a day before starting this recipe. **Serves 4**

INGREDIENTS

10½ oz (300 g) salt cod fillet; this will yield 7–9 oz (200–250 g) of fish once cooked

1 white onion, roughly chopped

1 fresh bay leaf

4 cups (1 liter, 34 fl oz) milk

2 slices bread

canola oil (non-GMO), for drizzling

2 large heads of frisée (see glossary), outer leaves removed, then washed and torn

20 chives, washed and chopped

1 small handful chervil, picked and washed

1 small handful flat-leaf (Italian) parsley, washed

2 small shallots, sliced

3 oz (80 g) pecorino or Parmesan, grated

BACON VINAIGRETTE

4 oz (100 g) bacon or pancetta, finely chopped

2 shallots, finely diced

3 tablespoons (40 ml, 1½ fl oz) whiskey

3 tablespoons (40 ml, 1½ fl oz) sherry vinegar

4 drops of Tabasco, or other spicy chili sauce

6 drops of Worcestershire sauce

METHOD

Soak the cod in a bowl of cold water for 24 hours, changing the water three times.

Next day, rinse the cod under fresh cold water and place in a large pot. Add the onion, bay leaf, and milk, then top with water until the fish is fully submerged. Place over medium heat and gently bring to a simmer. Let simmer for 4–5 minutes, then turn off the heat and let the cod sit. You just want to poach it gently.

Meanwhile, preheat the oven to 400°F (200°C, Gas 6). Tear the bread into small chunks and drizzle with a little canola oil. Place on a baking tray and bake for 5–7 minutes, or until golden, but still soft in the middle. Remove your croutons from the oven and set aside.

Place the frisée, herbs, and shallot in a mixing bowl and set aside.

To make the dressing, place a frying pan over high heat. Add the bacon and toss for a few minutes, until it turns brown and is cooked. Add the shallot and cook for another 2 minutes. Now add the whiskey and bubble away until reduced to a glaze. Stir in the vinegar and ½ cup (4 fl oz) water, then leave to cook for 5 minutes, or until the liquid has a vinaigrette consistency. Add the Tabasco and Worcestershire sauce and set aside.

Using a slotted spoon, carefully remove the cod from the poaching liquid onto a tray. Flake all the meat into the salad, removing any bones and skin. Add your toasted croutons.

Dress the salad with some warm bacon vinaigrette. Place in a serving bowl, add a little more dressing, then scatter with pecorino and serve.

NOTE: For other tempting uses for the Bacon Vinaigrette, see the salad dressing family tree on page 81.

MID-SPRING

Driving through the countryside, the signs of new life are everywhere, from the lambs and calves in the fields to the wild apple trees all in bloom. In the garden, my bed of early beans are creeping up the pole, starting to show the first of themselves for me to pick; the brassicas are starting to go to seed, showing their wonderful flowers of yellow and white; the maple trees are back, full of life; and that damn lawn needs mowing; and I really should weed the dandelions out of the grass, which are showing their yellow heads or fluffy whites that as a kid I loved to blow while making a wish.

RECIPE:

ROAST BEEF LEFTOVERS, GREEN BEANS, WATERCRESS & PARMESAN

I would really like to do a book on what to do with leftovers. It would be pages of simple recipes without measurements—just ideas of how to pair leftovers with other ingredients to make great new dishes. For this one I would slice up any leftover roast beef into thin strips, place in a bowl, and mix with some seeded mustard, a little olive oil, and a good dash of balsamic. Blanch a handful of those small green beans, tear a small handful of watercress into the mix, and then shave some parmesan over, using a veggie peeler. Mix it all up, then either enjoy for lunch as a salad or between two slices of good bread that have been spread with the best butter.

AVOCADO, SWEET POTATO & WALNUT SALAD

Late in 2013 I had the pleasure of cooking at Bar Tartine in San Francisco, where I met the amazing cooking couple Nicolaus Balla and Cortney Burns. I dined at Bar Tartine the previous evening, and it was one of the best meals I have ever had—it was so damn tasty. This is a version of one of the salads I enjoyed there. **Serves 4 as a plated starter**

INGREDIENTS

2 sweet potatoes, about 11–12½ oz (300–350 g) each, scrubbed but not peeled

1 ripe avocado, peeled, pit removed, then sliced

1 small fennel bulb, cored and thinly sliced

2 tablespoons chopped walnuts

2 tablespoons chopped dill pickles

1 large handful mâche leaves (see glossary), washed

2 tablespoons dill leaves, washed

1 tablespoon flat-leaf (Italian) parsley leaves, washed

2 oz (50 g) pecorino or hard salted ricotta (see glossary)

LEMON & WALNUT DRESSING

juice of 2 lemons

½ cup (100 ml, 4 fl oz) grapeseed oil, or canola oil (non-GMO)

3 tablespoons (40 ml, 1½ fl oz) walnut oil

1 tablespoon honey, warmed

1 garlic clove, finely chopped

salt

METHOD

Preheat the oven to 400°F (200°C, Gas 6). Stab the sweet potatoes all over, place on a baking tray, and roast for 30–50 minutes, or until you can insert a skewer through them. Let cool, then peel off the skin and cut the sweet potatoes into rounds.

To make the dressing, whisk all the ingredients together, then season to taste with salt.

To serve, arrange the sweet potato and avocado around a plate. Lightly dress the fennel with some of the dressing and arrange on the plate. Layer with walnuts and dill pickles. Dress with some more dressing.

In a bowl, combine the mâche, dill, and parsley. Dress lightly, then use to top the salad. Grate the pecorino all over, using a microplane. Serve immediately.

THE MRS.' TOASTED COUSCOUS SALAD

A little note from the boss: "We usually eat this at home as an accompaniment to schnitzel, homemade fish fingers, or a tagine. I vary the nuts and seeds based on whatever is in the cupboard. BMW (before Matt Wilkinson) I always used to add pine nuts, but he doesn't really like them!"—SG.

This dish could also be a main meal—just add roast veggies. **Serves 2**

INGREDIENTS

2 tablespoons (20 ml, 1 fl oz) olive oil, plus extra for drizzling

1 cup (185 g, 7 oz) instant couscous

¼ cup (40 g, 1½ oz) almonds, roughly chopped

1 tablespoon sunflower seeds, lightly toasted

1 tablespoon sesame seeds, lightly toasted

¼ cup (30 g, 1 oz) sultanas (golden raisins)

3½ oz (100 g) soft marinated feta, crumbled

juice of ½ lemon

10 chives, washed and finely chopped

1 small handful flat-leaf (Italian) parsley leaves, washed and chopped

METHOD

Heat the oil in a frying pan over medium heat. Add the couscous and toast for 5 minutes, or until the grains turn a light golden brown. Tip the couscous into a deep large bowl.

Pour over 1 cup (240 ml, 8 fl oz) boiling water, then cover with plastic wrap and let sit for 10 minutes. Remove the plastic and fluff the grains using a fork, until all the grains are separated and there are no clumps.

Add all the remaining ingredients and season with salt and freshly ground black pepper. Mix carefully but thoroughly, then taste—you may need to add an extra splash of olive oil to moisten the couscous a little. Serve.

G&T DRUNKEN CHICKEN WITH CARROTS & DUKKAH

A simple way to poach chicken, really playing on the Chinese version of drunken chicken, but with an English twist. Please note—sipping an actual gin and tonic while making this dish is a must.
Serves 2, plated or sharing

INGREDIENTS

2 free-range boneless, skinless chicken breasts, weighing 8 oz (230 g) each (see note), each cut into thirds lengthways

¾ cup plus 2 tablespoons (200 ml, 7 fl oz) gin

1 tablespoon salt

1 tablespoon sugar

1 star anise

6 dried juniper berries

3 pieces of dried mandarin peel, or fresh orange or lemon peel (without any bitter white pith)

3¼ cups (800 ml, 27 fl oz) tonic water

8 baby carrots, washed well, then cut in half lengthways

3 radicchio leaves, washed and shredded

4 large sorrel leaves (see glossary), washed and thinly sliced

2 spring onions (scallions), thinly sliced

1 teaspoon pickled ginger (from a jar), finely chopped

drizzle of olive oil

salt to taste

freshly ground black pepper

2 tablespoons Dukkah (see page 30)

METHOD

Place the chicken in a bowl that is large enough to hold up to 12 cups (3 liters, 101 fl oz) of liquid.

In an 8-cup (2 liter, 68 fl oz) saucepan, bring to a boil the gin, salt, sugar, spices, and mandarin peel. Take off the heat, stir in the tonic water, and let sit until cool. Pour the cooled liquid over the chicken, then cover and marinate in the fridge for 1–2 hours.

Leaving the chicken in the bowl, strain the marinating liquid back into the saucepan. Bring the liquid to a boil, then turn off the heat. While the liquid is very hot, add the chicken. Cover with a lid and leave for 20 minutes. Check that the chicken is cooked through; if it isn't, let it poach for another 5 minutes or so.

Remove the chicken from the liquid and place in the fridge to cool. Once cool, pull the chicken into long, fine shreds and place in a mixing bowl.

Wash out the saucepan, half-fill with water, and bring to a boil. Add the carrots and cook for 4–5 minutes, or until tender. Strain and add to the chicken.

Mix the radicchio, sorrel, spring onion, and pickled ginger with the chicken. Drizzle with olive oil, season with salt and freshly ground black pepper, then place in a serving bowl. Sprinkle with the dukkah ... and ka-pow!

NOTE: The weight of the chicken breast is important because it must cook through in this gentle poaching method.

PICKLED OCTOPUS, AVOCADO & CAULIFLOWER SALAD

I remember going to my Aunty Pat's house in the Canary Islands and having pickled octopus—or *pulpo* as it's known there—for the first time. It left me addicted. The combination of the pickled octopus, earthy cauliflower, and avocado cream is a dream for me. **Serves 4**

INGREDIENTS

1 lb 2 oz (500 g) octopus tentacles, cleaned and chopped into ⅜-inch (1 cm) pieces

3 garlic cloves, thinly sliced

1 large shallot, diced

1 small baby fennel bulb, cut in half, then finely diced

1¼ cups (340 ml, 11 fl oz) olive oil, plus extra for drizzling

½ cup (100 ml, 4 fl oz) red wine vinegar, or any other good vinegar

pinch of sugar

1 small cauliflower

2 oz (60 g) blanched almonds

1 teaspoon garam masala

5 sorrel leaves (see glossary), washed

1 small handful chopped flat-leaf (Italian) parsley

AVOCADO CREAM

1 ripe avocado, peeled, pit removed

1 tablespoon crème fraîche or sour cream

juice of 1 lemon

salt to taste

freshly ground black pepper

METHOD

Pour 4 cups (1 liter, 34 fl oz) water into a bowl. Add about 20 ice cubes to make an ice bath and set aside.

In a pot that can hold at least 12 cups (3 liters, 101 fl oz), bring 8 cups (2 liters, 68 fl oz) water to a boil. Add the octopus and cook for 1 minute. Strain off the water and plunge the octopus into the ice bath.

Bring fresh water to a boil in the saucepan. Carefully take the octopus out of its ice bath, put it back into the boiling water for another 20 seconds, then put it back into the ice bath.

Quickly make a pickling liquid by combining the garlic, shallot, fennel, olive oil, vinegar, and sugar in a bowl, then gently warming it in a pot. Submerge the octopus in the pickling liquid, then cover and refrigerate for a few hours. It's better to marinate the octopus overnight, but a couple of hours will do.

Preheat the oven to 425°F (220°C, Gas 7). Cut the cauliflower into florets about the size of a quarter. Place on a baking tray with the almonds and garam masala, drizzle with olive oil, then bake for 15–18 minutes, shaking the tray every 3 minutes or so, until the cauliflower is cooked and lightly brown. Tip the mixture into a large mixing bowl.

Gently warm the octopus. Using a slotted spoon, add the octopus and pickled vegetables to the cauliflower mixture. Toss to combine, then dress with a little of the pickling liquid. Mix the sorrel and parsley through and divide among serving bowls.

Blitz together the avocado cream ingredients with some salt and freshly ground black pepper. Add a dollop to each salad. Done.

NOODLES WITH FAVA BEANS, PEAS & SPICY LEMON DRESSING

There is something so refreshing about this salad. It's the perfect lunch dish for me—healthy, clean, and filling. Add a little fried tofu or some poached chicken if you like. **Serves 2 adults and 2 little hooligans**

INGREDIENTS

9½ oz (270 g) packet organic udon noodles

1 cup (175 g, 6 oz) shelled fresh fava (broad) beans

1 cup (175 g, 6½ oz) shelled fresh peas

2 tablespoons sesame seeds, lightly toasted

4 spring onions (scallions), thinly sliced; make sure you use some of the nice green tops too

SPICY LEMON DRESSING

juice of 1 lemon

2 tablespoons (20 ml, 1 fl oz) rice wine vinegar

¼ cup (50 ml, 2 fl oz) soy sauce

1 garlic clove, crushed

1 teaspoon chili paste (I like using an XO paste)

1 teaspoon salt

⅔ cup (150 ml, 5 fl oz) grapeseed oil, or canola oil (non-GMO)

METHOD

Bring a large pot of water to a boil. Add the noodles and cook for 10 minutes, then strain and rinse under cold water until cool.

Meanwhile, bring a smaller pot of water to a boil. Add the fava beans and cook for 1–2 minutes. Remove using a slotted spoon and refresh under cold water. When the fava beans are cool enough to handle, gently squeeze them out of their leathery skins.

Add the peas to the same pot of water the beans were cooked in. Cook for 2–3 minutes, or until just tender. Drain and set aside.

Make sure the noodles are dry, then place in a bowl. Add the peas, fava beans, half the sesame seeds, and half the spring onion.

Mix all the dressing ingredients in a small bowl until fully combined.

Drizzle the noodles with the dressing, coating everything. Top with the remaining sesame seeds and spring onion and serve.

LATE SPRING

I have bombarded the garden with tomato, chili, and eggplant seedlings; the basil is in, as are the cucumber seeds in a tray. I hope for an earlier crop than last year, but Mother Nature will let me know soon enough if I got it right.

My chickpeas are ready for the harvest, to be eaten like a pea—a love affair that has been going on for four years now, trying to understand crops that we generally only know of as dried legumes and grains, to see what they taste like fresh. Chickpeas are a brilliant source of nitrogen for the soil, so once picked, they will be turned back into the soil, ready for the late summer plants to go in.

RECIPE:

FRESH CHICKPEA SALAD

If you don't have fresh chickpeas, substitute with green English peas or fava (broad) beans. Grab yourself a good-size bowl full of the pods, and then slip them out of the pods; hopefully, you'll end up with a good cup or two of fresh legumes. Keep half of them raw, blanch the others in boiling water until just tender, then mix them all together. You could shave some raw asparagus through, if you have some on hand (I would!). To this, add a peeled and shaved shallot, and some crumbled feta. To dress the salad, you could use the Caper & Raisin Dressing on page 77 or the Simple Lemon Dressing on page 24. Enjoy on toast with a poached egg, or serve alongside some steamed fish.

WARM SALAD OF KING BROWN MUSHROOMS, ASPARAGUS & FAVA BEANS

Here's a truly wonderful warm salad with a great cheesy dressing. It should be enjoyed with a good glass of vino and bread to mop up with after. **Serves 2–4 sharing**

INGREDIENTS

8–10 asparagus spears, woody ends trimmed, stalks peeled up to the tips

1 cup (175 g, about 6 oz) fresh tiny fava (broad) beans, in their pods

½ cup (80 g, 2¾ oz) shelled fresh peas

1 tablespoon butter

¼ cup (50 ml, 2 fl oz) olive oil

4 king brown or oyster mushrooms, cut in half lengthways

1 oz (30 g) gorgonzola, diced or crumbled

1 tablespoon mascarpone

1 large handful mâche (lamb's lettuce) leaves (see glossary), washed

1 shallot, sliced

1 small handful flat-leaf (Italian) parsley leaves, washed and chopped

METHOD

Bring a pot of water to a boil. Cut the asparagus spears in half so one bit has the tip, the other is just the stalk. Place in a bowl with the fava beans and peas. Add the greens to the boiling water and cook for 1½ minutes. Strain, then set aside.

Meanwhile, heat the butter and olive oil in a frying pan and gently sauté the mushrooms, cut side facing down. Add ⅔ cups (150 ml) water and cook for 2–3 minutes, or until the mushrooms are tender. Strain the liquid through a sieve into a small pot, and set aside. Add the mushrooms to the blanched asparagus, beans, and peas.

Add the gorgonzola and mascarpone to the mushroom liquid and bring to a boil. Once the cheeses start to melt, turn up the heat, stir in another ¼ cup (50 ml, 2 fl oz) hot water to help it all emulsify, then season with salt and freshly ground black pepper.

Add the mâche, shallot, and parsley to the mushroom salad. Arrange on a serving platter, drizzle with the hot cheesy dressing, and enjoy.

Spring is the pinnacle of good pasture for farmers, after the paddocks have woken up from their winter dormancy, when the ground has thawed and softened.

GRILLED WHITING WITH CAPER & RAISIN DRESSING

I have adapted a memory from my childhood here for this dish, using whiting instead of sardines—but please, if you have amazing sardines or mullet, adapt the recipe to suit. I fondly remember being on the Algarve in Portugal with my dad and grandad, eating for the first time some fantastic fresh, huge sardines, served with a simple salad, bread, and, of course, some sangria and an icy cold beer. **Serves 4**

INGREDIENTS

4 large whiting (or cod, hake, or sole), filleted and pin-boned; ask your fishmonger to do this for you

¼ cup (50 ml, 2 fl oz) olive oil

zest of 1 lemon

salt to taste

freshly ground black pepper

1 big handful arugula (rocket) leaves, washed

5½ oz (150 g) Greek-style feta, crumbled

2 tablespoons toasted pine nuts

CAPER & RAISIN DRESSING

1 tablespoon raisins, soaked in water for 5 minutes, then drained

1 tablespoon salted capers, rinsed

3 anchovy fillets

1 small sweet red chili, seeded and finely chopped

1 garlic clove, crushed

5 basil leaves, washed and finely chopped

2 tablespoons (20 ml, 1 fl oz) balsamic vinegar

juice of 1 lemon

salt to taste

freshly ground black pepper

1 cup (250 ml, 8 fl oz) olive oil

METHOD

Turn on the broiler (oven grill) to full heat; if you don't have a broiler, heat up the oven until it is really hot.

Meanwhile, lay the whiting fillets on a baking tray, spreading them out so they're not touching. Mix together the olive oil, lemon zest, and some salt and freshly ground black pepper. Spread the mixture over the fish and let sit while you make the dressing.

Using a mortar and pestle, pound the raisins, capers, anchovies, chili, garlic, and basil to a sticky paste consistency. Add the vinegar and lemon juice, some salt and freshly ground black pepper, then fold the olive oil through.

Lay most of the arugula on a serving platter or on individual plates, and drizzle with a little of the dressing.

Broil the whiting for 3–5 minutes, or until crispy on top and cooked through. Pour the cooking juices over the arugula, then arrange the whiting fillets over the top. Drizzle some more dressing over each whiting fillet. Scatter with the feta, pine nuts, and remaining arugula.

Hope you have a glass of sangria in your hand while you're enjoying this dish ...

NOTE: See the dressing family tree on page 81 for other luscious ways with the Caper & Raisin Dressing.

SALAD OF BEANS WITH HONEY DRESSING & SMOKED ALMONDS

Over the past few years I have had more success in growing beans at home. I now mix it up a little bit, growing bush varieties of beans and some that need a trellis. I'm also addicted to smoked almonds—a great little snack just on their own. **Serves 4 sharing**

INGREDIENTS

10½ oz (300 g) green beans, trimmed

10½ oz (300 g) lima beans, trimmed

10½ oz (300 g) flat green beans (also known as Spanish flat beans or Roman beans), trimmed

1 small handful flat-leaf (Italian) parsley, washed and torn

1 small handful mint, washed and roughly chopped

2 shallots, thinly sliced

HONEY DRESSING

¼ cup (90 g, 3 oz) honey

⅓ cup (50 g, 1¾ oz) smoked almonds (sold in health food shops and Middle Eastern markets), chopped

½ cup (100 ml, 4 fl oz) olive oil

¼ cup (50 ml, 2 fl oz) sherry vinegar

METHOD

Bring a large pot of water to the boil. Add all the beans and cook for 2–3 minutes. Test to see if they're cooked by scooping one out of the water and biting into it—you're looking for a little crunch to still be there. Once done, drain the beans in a colander and refresh under cold water until cool. Set aside.

To make the dressing, add the honey and almonds to a little pot and warm gently over low heat. Add the olive oil and vinegar and take off the heat.

Place the beans in a mixing bowl, add the herbs and shallots, then add the dressing. Mix together, then serve on your desired plates or in shallow bowls.

SPRING

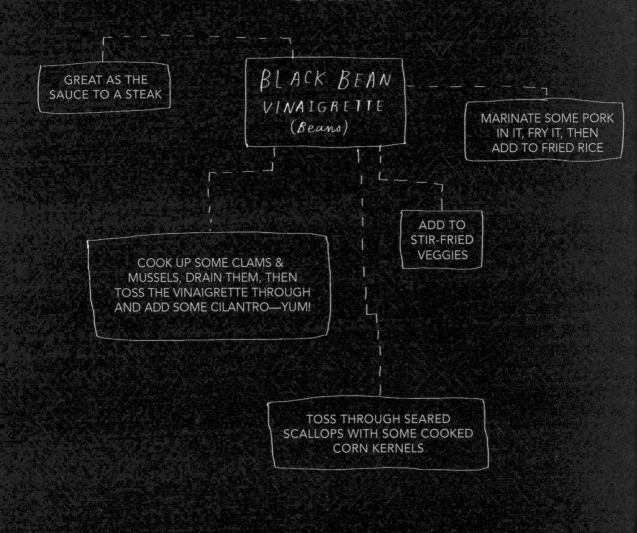

GREAT AS THE
SAUCE TO A STEAK

BLACK BEAN
VINAIGRETTE
(Beans)

MARINATE SOME PORK
IN IT, FRY IT, THEN
ADD TO FRIED RICE

ADD TO
STIR-FRIED
VEGGIES

COOK UP SOME CLAMS &
MUSSELS, DRAIN THEM, THEN
TOSS THE VINAIGRETTE THROUGH
AND ADD SOME CILANTRO—YUM!

TOSS THROUGH SEARED
SCALLOPS WITH SOME COOKED
CORN KERNELS

SUPER DRESSING FOR
ROASTED QUAIL

TOSS THROUGH WARM
POTATOES AS AN EASY
SALAD

SPRING

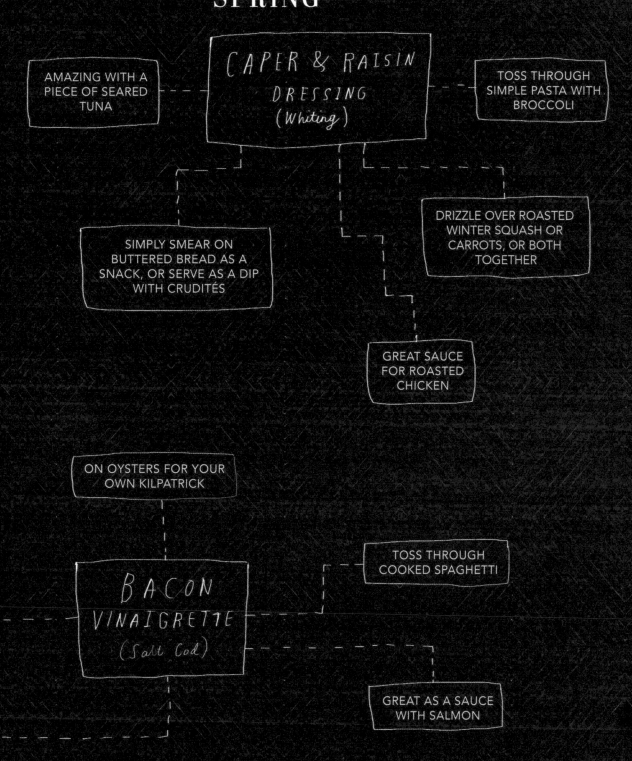

CAPER & RAISIN DRESSING
(Whiting)

AMAZING WITH A PIECE OF SEARED TUNA

TOSS THROUGH SIMPLE PASTA WITH BROCCOLI

SIMPLY SMEAR ON BUTTERED BREAD AS A SNACK, OR SERVE AS A DIP WITH CRUDITÉS

DRIZZLE OVER ROASTED WINTER SQUASH OR CARROTS, OR BOTH TOGETHER

GREAT SAUCE FOR ROASTED CHICKEN

ON OYSTERS FOR YOUR OWN KILPATRICK

TOSS THROUGH COOKED SPAGHETTI

BACON VINAIGRETTE
(Salt Cod)

GREAT AS A SAUCE WITH SALMON

PINEAPPLE, MINT & COCONUT SALAD

I love it when the tropical fruits come into season. It makes me want to go laze on a beach somewhere warm, eat fruit, and drink cocktails with crazy things hanging out of the glass. **Serves 4**

INGREDIENTS

1 pineapple, peeled, cored, and cut into long "finger" wedges

3 tablespoons (50 g, 2 oz) coconut sugar (available from health food stores)

2 teaspoons (5 g, ¼ oz) salt

1 cup (125 g, 4 oz) dried mint leaves, roughly chopped

1 teaspoon whole white peppercorns

flesh of ½ fresh young coconut, well chilled

small mint leaves, to garnish

METHOD

Lay the pineapple wedges on a serving plate.

Using a mortar and pestle, grind together the coconut sugar, salt, dried mint, and peppercorns. Sprinkle the mixture all over the pineapple, then scatter with the fresh mint leaves.

Cut the coconut flesh into thin strips and arrange over the top.

Eat with your hands, making sure you get the fresh coconut too!

LEMON
VERBENA
CORDIAL

INGREDIENTS

4 cups (750g, 1lb 11oz) sugar

1 tablespoon (15g, ½ oz)
citric acid (see glossary)

½ oz (15g) or 60 lemon
verbena leaves

LEMON VERBENA CORDIAL

If you don't have a lemon verbena plant in your garden or on your balcony, then you should. Its aroma is stunning, and it's brilliant as a fresh herbal tea or infused into cream-based desserts. One of those clever South American–origin plants that does really well elsewhere. **Makes 4 cups (1 liter, 34 fl oz)**

METHOD

Put the sugar and citric acid in a pot with 4 cups (1 liter, 34 fl oz) water. Bring to a boil over medium heat, stirring to make sure the sugar has dissolved.

Place the lemon verbena leaves in a heatproof bowl and pour the hot liquid over them. Cover and leave to infuse at room temperature until cool.

Pour the liquid through a fine sieve into a clean pot. Bring back to a boil, then pour into sterilized jars and seal.

Keep in a cool dark place for up to 6 months. Once opened, store in the fridge for up to 8 weeks.

ELDER-
FLOWER
CORDIAL

INGREDIENTS

4 cups (750g, 1lb 11oz) sugar

1 tablespoon (15g, ½ oz)
citric acid (see glossary)

25 elderflower heads, tips
and flowers only, washed

ELDERFLOWER CORDIAL

I have many fond memories of elderflower and its berries as a child, and have rediscovered it over the past few years. The flowers make the best cordial ever! This cordial is great to use as a dressing or to finish a sauce, such as a chicken gravy. **Makes about 4 cups (1 liter, 34 fl oz)**

METHOD

Put the sugar and citric acid in a pot with 4 cups (1 liter, 34 fl oz) water. Bring to a boil over medium heat, stirring to make sure the sugar has dissolved.

Place the elderflower tips and flowers in a heatproof bowl and pour the hot liquid over them. Cover and leave to infuse at room temperature until cool.

Pour the liquid through a fine sieve into a clean pot. Bring back to a boil, then pour into sterilized jars and seal.

Keep in a cool dark place for up to 6 months. Once opened, store in the fridge for up to 8 weeks.

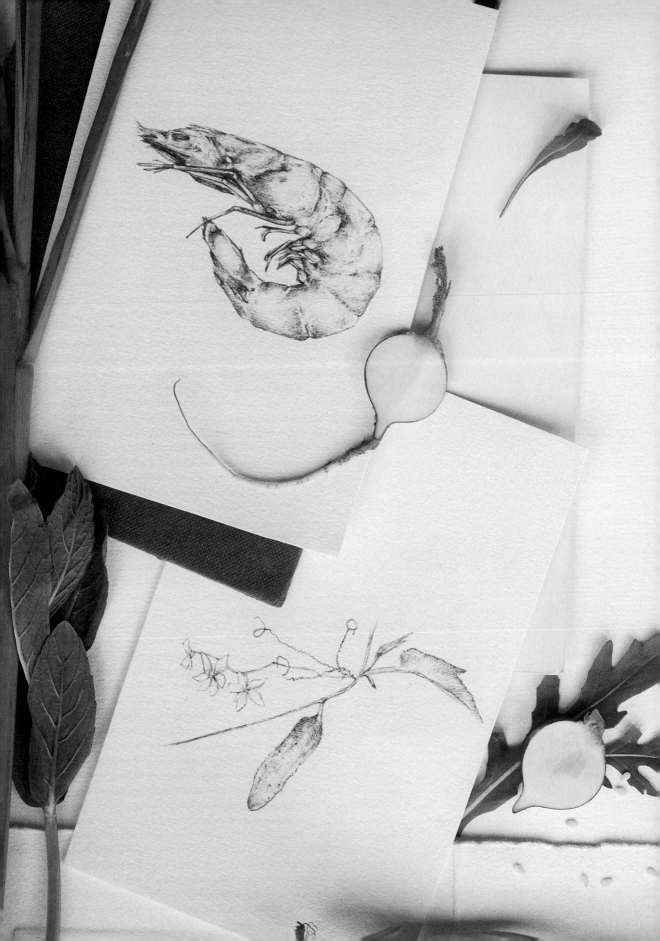

SUMMER

SUMMER

I HAVE TO ADMIT IT: SUMMER IS MY FAVORITE SEASON. I THOUGHT MAYBE IT WAS AUTUMN FOR A WHILE, AND EVEN WINTER, BUT UPON REFLECTION IT HAS TO BE SUMMER, DOESN'T IT?

Warm days, long nights … summer is three months of outdoor eating and the beach, enjoying the open air and being near water. I hate sand, but summer makes you all nostalgic for the feeling of sand on your bare feet, all in between your toes, memories of being at the beach as a kid with all the extended family, getting sunburnt, and drinking homemade cordial on ice. There is a warmth to the air that carries the smell of barbecues, of meat fat dripping onto embers, of coconut suntan lotion, and the smell of the tomato vine. That smell always reminds me of my Granddad Tom, the man who first taught me about seasonality and gave me my love of gardening.

We change our habits in summer. We stop hibernating and get outside. We see friends for afternoon drinks, and there is nothing finer than a crisp cold beer or a gin and tonic or even a Pimm's, after a day in the garden. Even the English are happy in summer.

We cook over coals, and eat messy foods with our hands—I'm thinking of peeling shrimp with your hands or biting into a juicy stonefruit or a ripe tomato … and of course, that epitome of both summer fruit and juicy mess, the mango! There's nothing like getting stuck into a gorgeous ripe mango cheek and having the juice running down your chin. Summer is just messy. It's juicy berries and cherries just waiting to stain your mouth and your hands and your clothes.

And in the garden it's so delightful to pick things off the stalk or the vine, all warmed by the sun, and eat them raw, right there and then. Everything is standing proud, buoyed up with all that sunshine, and a little bit of water. My favorite is to pick a cob of corn straight off the stalk, peel back the skin, and just bite into it. It is just delicious as a raw vegetable and unbelievably sweet.

Summer to me is all about food that is easy and fresh—"throw together" kind of stuff. The abundance of everything makes it easy to create simple and good-for-you "fast food." The garden is like a big "pick and mix" when it comes to getting inspired for dinner. Grate and lightly salt a zucchini for an instant salad base. Throw some tomatoes on a plate with torn basil and some mozzarella. Add seasoning, olive oil, and a splash of nice sherry vinegar, and you're done. Pick your corn and throw it straight on the barbecue. Having casual meals with your mates is easier to do in summer because we are spoiled with choice. There is double the amount of fresh seasonal produce available in summer than there is in autumn, for example.

Historically, the summer solstice—the longest day of the year—has been celebrated as a holy day since pagan times, and is called 'midsummer' in many cultures across Europe and beyond. Many countries still mark the occasion with bonfires to light the night and symbolically keep the evil spirits away, and to also mark the fertility of the season and ask for a successful harvest. Not a bad reason for a bonfire, really.

The garden in summer is an everyday affair for me. I either get out there early, just as the sun is rising, or in the early evening, making sure I give everything a good soaking and seeing that nothing is getting scorched by the sun. You need to keep an eye on things and do a bit of maintenance, like tying up all your tomatoes, to give the plants the best chance. Things shoot up so quickly with all the sunlight that you really want to keep a close eye, especially on your salad leaves, which are likely to bolt to seed given a chance and become quite bitter. To combat this, drape a piece of shade cloth over them to protect them from the fierce midday sun.

Every year I try to grow squash in summer too. Don't ask me why, as I never seem to get any. The vines disappear over the fence and the neighbors get all the bounty. Every time! Oh, well. It's nice to share.

It's also a lovely time for flowers in the garden. The butterflies and bees are flitting around; the roses are blooming, and the sunflowers sway in the breeze. It is one of the simplest and most rewarding ways to get your kids into the garden with you, and get them excited about what they can plant and grow. Put in some sunflower seeds, and watch them stretch up into the sky. The kids will be so delighted to know that something so big came from the tiny seed they planted themselves.

Indulge in cherry season. It's so short, I end up on security duty, watching out my window and keeping an eye on our cherry tree day by day, just wanting to beat the birds to the fruit. But cherries are such a delight, if you can get some at your farmers' market, then please do. They are summer in a bowl.

We stop hibernating and get outside. We see friends for afternoon drinks, and there is nothing finer than a crisp cold beer or a gin and tonic or even a Pimm's, after a day in the garden.

ZUCCHINI WITH AJO BLANCO DRESSING & SPICED NUTS

Over the last few years I have started to love zucchini, but I have to admit that by the end of the season, it's like, "Not *another* bloody zucchini!" That said, this is one of the joys of eating seasonally—anticipation and excitement at the start of the season, despair and overload at the end. **Serves 2 as a large share, or 4 smaller servings**

INGREDIENTS

1 lb 4 oz (600 g) mixed heirloom zucchini (courgettes), cut into random pieces

½ cup (100 ml, 4 fl oz) extra-virgin olive oil

½ oz (15 g) hazelnuts, chopped

½ oz (15 g) blanched almonds, chopped

½ oz (15 g) walnuts, chopped

pinch of smoked paprika

salt to taste

1 small handful flat-leaf (Italian) parsley, washed and chopped

1 small handful mint, washed and chopped

freshly ground black pepper

AJO BLANCO DRESSING

3 to 4 slices white bread (75 g, 2¾ oz), crusts removed

¾ cup (115 g, 4 oz) blanched almonds, roughly chopped

1 garlic clove, peeled

1 teaspoon sherry vinegar

½ cup (100 ml, 4 fl oz) extra-virgin olive oil

⅓ cup (80 ml, 2½ fl oz) ice-cold water

salt to taste

METHOD

For the dressing, first soak the bread in water for 5 minutes. Drain the bread, then place in a blender with the almonds, garlic, vinegar, and olive oil. Gradually add the cold water and blend on high for 30 seconds, or until a smooth purée forms. Add salt to taste, then set aside in a bowl until serving time.

Preheat the oven to 350°F (180°C, Gas 4), and heat a ridged grill pan or grill to high, until slightly smoky.

Coat the cut sides of the zucchini pieces with ⅓ cup (80 ml, 2½ fl oz) of the olive oil. Place them on the ridged grill pan and cook them, turning now and then, until they are branded all over. Place on a baking tray and finish in the oven for another 3–5 minutes—you want to cook them through, but leave a bit of texture and crunch to the zucchini. Once cooked, set aside and keep warm.

Place the nuts and remaining olive oil in a small saucepan over medium heat and warm through until fragrant. Transfer the nuts to a bowl, then season with the paprika and salt to taste.

To assemble the dish, place the warm zucchini in a large mixing bowl, along with the herbs and nuts, and stir gently to combine. Season with salt to taste and freshly ground black pepper if needed.

Dollop most of the dressing around the bottom of your serving dish, then arrange the zucchini salad on top. If desired, drizzle some more dressing on top for that creamy, nutty flavor and texture.

WATERMELON & FETA WITH SHRIMP VINAIGRETTE

When I first heard of watermelon with feta, I was quite disgusted. "Filthy buggers!" I thought—that is, until I tried it. This salad is delicious on its own, but add this warm shrimp vinaigrette to it and you have a stunning dish. **Serves 4**

INGREDIENTS

1 lb 2 oz (500 g) watermelon, peeled and cut into 1¼-inch (3 cm) cubes

3½ oz (100 g) feta, broken into thumbnail-sized pieces

8 mint leaves, washed

5 basil leaves, washed

SHRIMP VINAIGRETTE

½ cup (100 ml, 4 fl oz) olive oil

9 oz (250 g) raw shrimp (prawns), peeled, deveined, and roughly chopped

1 shallot, finely diced

2 garlic cloves, sliced

1 red birdseye (red bullet) chili, seeded and thinly sliced

1 tablespoon tomato paste (concentrated purée)

3 tablespoons (40 ml, 1½ fl oz) sherry vinegar

⅔ cup plus 1 tablespoon (160 ml, 5½ fl oz) verjuice or white wine

1 tablespoon salted baby capers, rinsed

METHOD

Start by making the vinaigrette. Heat a saucepan over high heat. Add a little of the olive oil and when hot, add the shrimp. Cook for 2–4 minutes, until the shrimp are a little colored, then add the shallot, garlic, and chili. Turn the heat down to medium and cook, gently stirring, for 3–4 minutes, until the shallot starts to sweat but not color.

Add the tomato paste and vinegar and cook for a few minutes, until fully incorporated. Stir in the verjuice, bring to a boil, then allow to reduce for 3–5 minutes, until the liquid forms a glaze. Add the capers, stir in the rest of the olive oil, then take off the heat.

Arrange the watermelon pieces in your serving bowl, then spoon the vinaigrette over. You may not need to use all the vinaigrette, so store the rest in an airtight container in the fridge; it will keep for up to 5 days.

Scatter the feta over the watermelon, tear the mint and basil all over, and serve.

NOTE: For other winning ways with your wonderful Shrimp Vinaigrette, see the salad dressing family tree on page 130.

GRILLED PEACHES & CHICKEN WITH ARUGULA & KASUNDI

This is a stand-alone salad. I adore the thought of it gracing the middle of an outdoor table during a nice little summer lunch with friends or family, with some crusty bread and a few glasses of wine.
Serves 4–6 sharing

INGREDIENTS

6 boneless, skinless free-range chicken thighs

1¼ cups (280 g, 10 oz) plain yogurt

2 tablespoons Tomato Kasundi (see page 33)

3 firm peaches, each cut into 8 wedges, leaving the skin on

½ cup (100 ml, 4 fl oz) olive oil

pinch of ras el hanout (see glossary)

1 large handful arugula (rocket) leaves, washed

METHOD

Place the chicken in a bowl. Mix the yogurt and kasundi together. Reserve 2 tablespoons to dollop over the salad, then thoroughly mix the remaining yogurt mixture with the chicken. Cover and marinate in the fridge—overnight if you can. If not, an hour or so is good, but if you haven't time, then I guess just go for it.

Heat a ridged grill pan or the grill to high.

Meanwhile, take the peaches and gently mix in a bowl with the olive oil and ras el hanout. Cook on the pan or grill for about 1 minute on each side, until the skins on the edge start to split—you want the peaches to be cooked but not mushy. Place back in the bowl and cover with a plate.

Now grill your chicken on each side until cooked, about 7–10 minutes. Place on a board and cut each thigh into about eight slices.

Mix the chicken with the peaches. Throw in the arugula, toss gently, then transfer straight away to a serving bowl or platter. Spoon the reserved kasundi and yogurt mixture on top and serve.

EARLY SUMMER

Early summer is the time to find those shorts that have been hidden away in a drawer or the cupboard, scrub the grill, make sure your watering system in the garden is working properly, and ensure you have a good supply of cold beverages in the house ... ideally beer!

It's time to plant those sunflower seeds that give the kids so much joy, and stake the tomatoes and anything else that will need taming through the next few months. Early summer is a vast array of green and flowers. I love it, but it's still that in-between season—not quite too hot yet, but getting there.

LEFTOVER CHICKEN TURNED INTO CORONATION DELIGHT

Leftover chicken has so many uses, I almost don't know where to start. Take said leftover chicken, pick off all the flesh, and roughly chop. To this, add some mayonnaise to bind it, and some great quality madras curry paste. Now some may laugh about this, especially a chef hero who will not be named, but there are some really good premade pastes on the market now, so that's what I would use. Add enough to your liking, mix through some nice golden raisins, roasted flaked almonds, and lots of chopped fresh cilantro leaves for a great little salad. You could chop up and roast some sweet potatoes or squash to add to this dish, which will only make it more special.

MISO-GLAZED EGGPLANT WITH PICKLED GINGER & SPRING ONION

In 2007 I had this most memorable meal in Tokyo. We were greeted at the restaurant door by the manager, who asked if we spoke Japanese. Obviously not, but his words were, "It's okay, I speak English!" He lied, but it turned out to be a fun-filled night of great food and lots of sake. I had something like this, but grilled in a wood-fired oven and served with mashed foie gras. **Serves 2–4 sharing**

INGREDIENTS

2 large eggplants (aubergines), cut in half, then flesh scored all over in a crisscross pattern

canola oil (non-GMO), for brushing

2 tablespoons (20 ml, 1 fl oz) mirin

2 tablespoons yellow miso paste

1 teaspoon superfine (caster) sugar

1 teaspoon Japanese chili flakes (these are a bit finer than regular chili flakes, but you can use the regular ones instead)

2 teaspoons white sesame seeds, half of them lightly toasted for garnishing

2 tablespoons (20 ml, 1 fl oz) white sesame oil (see glossary; please try to get white sesame oil for this dish, or use a good quality regular sesame oil)

1 teaspoon rice wine vinegar

2 spring onions (scallions), white and green bits separated, then thinly sliced

1 teaspoon pickled ginger (from a jar), finely chopped

10½ oz (300 g) organic silken tofu, cut into 12 portions

METHOD

Preheat the oven to 375°F (190°C, Gas 5). Place the eggplants on a large baking tray, skin side down, and brush with some canola oil. Cover the tray with foil and bake the eggplants for 40–60 minutes, or until a skewer can be inserted through easily.

Remove from the oven and leave until cool enough to handle. Being careful not to break the skin, scoop the eggplant flesh into a bowl. Place the eggplant shells on the baking tray, on their backs, ready to hold the filling.

Break up the eggplant flesh by mixing it with the mirin, miso paste, sugar, chili flakes, untoasted sesame seeds, sesame oil, rice wine vinegar, white spring onion bits, and pickled ginger. Gently fold in the tofu. Spoon the mixture into the eggplant shells and bake for a further 10 minutes, until all glazed.

Lay the filled eggplants on serving plates. Sprinkle with the toasted sesame seeds and bits of green spring onion. Serve warm.

The garden is like a big "pick and mix" when it comes to getting inspired for dinner. It is so delightful to pluck things off the stalk or the vine, all warmed by the sun, and eat them raw, right there and then.

ROASTED SWEET POTATOES WITH HOT RED TURKISH PEPPERS & LABNEH

You could add a few extra bits and bobs to this dish and you'll have yourself a posh baked sweet potato for dinner or lunch … but for me, this is simply a great shared salad. **Serves 4 sharing**

INGREDIENTS

4 sweet potatoes, about 10½–14 oz (300–400 g) (use the golden-skin variety), scrubbed

1 lemongrass stem, white part only, chopped

⅔ cup (150 ml, 5 fl oz) rice wine vinegar

¼ cup (50 g, 1¾ oz) superfine (caster) sugar

¾ cup (180 ml, 6 fl oz) grapeseed oil or canola oil (non-GMO)

2 shallots, finely diced

4½ oz (120 g) hot Turkish red peppers or piquillo peppers (see glossary), drained and sliced

⅔ cup plus 1 tablespoon (150 g, 5½ oz) labneh (thick Greek yogurt)

1 handful cilantro (coriander), leaves picked, washed and chopped

2 tablespoons Dukkah (see page 30)

METHOD

Preheat the oven to 400ºF (200ºC, Gas 6). Place the sweet potatoes on a baking tray. Using a small sharp knife, stab each one through the skin a few times, but watch ya fingers. Cover with foil and bake for 30–50 minutes, or until tender. (If you want a little cheat tip— but please don't tell the Mrs.!—first cook the sweet potatoes in the microwave for 12 minutes, then place in the hot oven for 8–10 minutes. I've been getting away with cooking all spuds like this for years without the Mrs. knowing about it …)

Meanwhile, in a small saucepan, bring the lemongrass, vinegar, and sugar to a boil, then remove from the heat. Let steep until the sweet potatoes are cooked.

Arrange the cooked sweet potatoes on a serving plate and leave to cool a little. Strain the lemongrass-infused vinegar into a bowl, whisk in the grapeseed oil, then add the shallot.

Tear open the sweet potatoes and drizzle with a little lemongrass dressing. Top with the red peppers, then spoon the labneh all over. Dress with a little more dressing, then finish with the cilantro, dressed in a little more of the dressing. Sprinkle with the dukkah and serve.

NOTE: Labneh is made by draining Greek yogurt until it's thick and tangy. You can buy it at Middle Eastern markets and health food stores.

SCORCHED TOMATOES WITH WHITE ANCHOVIES & SALTED RICOTTA

I was trying to have all the flavor of fresh tomatoes, but just a little cooked, yet not all mushy … which is how I came about cooking tomatoes this way. It intensifies their flavor and gives them a new taste and texture. **Serves 2–4 sharing**

INGREDIENTS

¼ cup (50 ml, 2 fl oz) olive oil

14 oz (400 g) baby roma (plum) tomatoes, or large cherry tomatoes

1½ oz (40 g) white anchovy fillets (see glossary)

2 tablespoons (20 ml, 1 fl oz) red wine vinegar

1¾ oz (50 g) salted ricotta (see glossary), or any similar hard cheese

8–10 small basil leaves, washed

METHOD

Place a large pot over a high heat. Add the olive oil and heat until hot. Add the tomatoes and shake the pot until the skins start to burst—about 30 seconds to 1 minute. As soon as you see the first skins burst, immediately pour the whole contents of the pot onto your serving plate. Let cool for 5 minutes.

Lay the anchovies over the tomatoes. Drizzle with the vinegar, then scatter the basil over. Microplane or finely grate the cheese all over the tomatoes and enjoy.

BAKED SNAPPER WITH FISH SAUCE DRESSING, CUCUMBER & MINT SALAD

A simple baked fish dish—but if you wanted, you could serve it equally as well as a marinated raw dish. Remove the skin from the fish, slice it small enough, and there's no need to actually cook the fish at all.

Serves 4 as a main course salad

INGREDIENTS

1 lb 5 oz (600 g) snapper fillet, scaled and pin-boned (ask your fishmonger to do this for you)

1 large grapefruit (any variety)

¼ cup (50 ml, 2 fl oz) fish sauce

¼ cup (50 ml, 2 fl oz) soy sauce

1 tablespoon superfine (caster) sugar

½ cup (100 ml, 4 fl oz) grapeseed oil or canola oil (non-GMO)

3 spring onions (scallions)

10 Vietnamese mint leaves, washed and chopped

4 flat-leaf (Italian) parsley stalks and leaves, washed and chopped

1 birdseye (bullet) chili, chopped (seeds and all!)

2 Lebanese (or other small short) cucumbers, thinly sliced lengthways, using a mandoline

1 handful cilantro (coriander), leaves picked and washed

1 small handful mint leaves, washed and torn

METHOD

Preheat the oven to 425ºF (220ºC, Gas 7). Cut the snapper fillet into eight pieces. Arrange the snapper portions in a baking dish, so no pieces are touching each other.

The grapefruit here is very important. First slice the top and bottom off using a sharp knife, then carefully remove the skin and the white pith, starting from the top and working down to the bottom, as if you are following the lines of a soccer ball. Once this is all done, and working over a bowl to catch all the juices, slice between each vein to get a perfect segment. Each segment we are going to cut into five portions and place in a dish for later; also reserve all the juice.

Pass the grapefruit juice through a sieve into a bowl. Whisk in the fish sauce, soy sauce, sugar, and grapeseed oil. Spoon half the dressing over the fish, then pop the fish in the oven for 15–18 minutes, or until cooked.

Chop the spring onions finely, placing the green parts into the remaining dressing mixture and the white bits in a separate bowl.

To the dressing, add the Vietnamese mint, parsley, chili and the grapefruit segments; set aside.

To the bowl with the white spring onion bits, add the cucumber, cilantro and mint, then dress with a little dressing.

Arrange the salad around a large shallow serving bowl or platter. Place the snapper portions on top, drizzle with as much dressing as you desire, then serve straight away.

MIDSUMMER

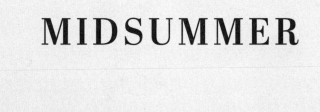

The waiting is over. At last it is here, what we have been waiting for all year—vast amounts of luscious produce to gorge upon. I again have a tomato in my hand, eating it, savoring that taste of summer. It's been a long wait for the taste of a real tomato since the end of their season last year; I have watched them grow in my garden, and they are now here for me to relish.

With the tomatoes come the cucumbers, zucchini, corn, eggplants—not to forget the peaches, plums, melons, and berries. Oh, the berries! So much to eat, so much to love. They don't even need cooking. Don't spoil the flavor, just simply enjoy most produce raw. This is the excitement of what seasonal eating gives. Forgive me if I sound a little crazed—it's simply just excitement at the thought of such great food!

RECIPE:

UNCLE FRANK'S CHOPPED SALAD

Aunty Jane and Uncle Frank played a massive role in my earlier life. Now, Uncle Frank is the gourmet of the family, and word on the street is that he is ready to give me a nudge. This is a play on a chopped salad, but it's damn tasty and resembles a little bit the salad I have as a memory from my early days working in the pub in Barnsley. Layer in a bowl, in this order: ½ inch (1 cm) strips of Boston or butter lettuce, torn mint, capers, a spoonful of sun-dried tomatoes, torn basil, a tablespoon each of sliced pickled garlic and onion, then 1 chopped pickled hot chilli. Using salad servers, mix thoroughly, then add splashes of good white wine vinegar and olive oil. Place in a serving bowl and sprinkle with salt and freshly ground black pepper. Top with shredded carrot and beet, some more capers, and some torn cilantro leaves. Then as Uncle Frank says, "Get stuck in, lovely!"

SALTED CUCUMBER WITH SESAME, GARLIC & VINEGAR

I have been trained in classic and modern French cookery, but over the years my repertoire has extended to many cuisines. I'll be honest: I'm not that good at Chinese or Southeast Asian cooking, but I practice a lot at home, using the family as guinea pigs. This is one of those simple recipes that turned out to be a ripper. **Serves 4**

INGREDIENTS

4 Lebanese (or other small short) cucumbers

1 tablespoon salt

½ cup (100 ml, 4 fl oz) sunflower or grapeseed oil

5 garlic cloves, finely diced

1 tablespoon sesame seeds

¼ cup (50 ml, 2 fl oz) chardonnay vinegar (see glossary)

METHOD

Peel your cucumbers, then slice them into rounds about the thickness of your pinky. Place in a colander, add the salt, stir thoroughly, and let sit for 10 minutes. Now wash under cold water and let drain for a bit.

Meanwhile, back at the ranch, place the sunflower oil and garlic in a small pot and bring to a simmer over medium heat. Now we are going to cook out the garlic until it starts to turn golden brown; once it has, take it off the heat, add the sesame seeds, then transfer to a bowl. Keep stirring for a bit until the mixture cools, then stir in the vinegar.

Dry off the cucumber, then toss with the garlic and sesame dressing. Place in your desired bowl and serve.

FOSSIE'S CHARRED CORN & POTATO SALAD

My business partner, Ben Foster, is a damn good cook. Don't tell him I said that, but he really is—although he's a bit messy in the kitchen, like all "home chef wannabes," hee hee hee. This is one of his staple summer/early autumn salads that I have enjoyed many a time at his house. **Serves 4, or 2 if you want some leftovers for lunch the next day**

INGREDIENTS

2 lb 3 oz (1 kg) boiling (waxy) potatoes, such as fingerling or small yellow finn or rose fir, peeled and roughly diced

2 ears corn, husked

½ cup (120 g, 4 oz) mayonnaise (see page 25 for a home made version)

¼ teaspoon chipotle chili powder

1 tablespoon chopped pickled jalapeño chilies

3 spring onions (scallions), chopped

1 small handful cilantro (coriander), leaves picked, washed, and chopped

juice of 1 lime

salt to taste

freshly ground black pepper

METHOD

Place the potatoes in a pot and cover with water. Bring to a boil and cook for 5–7 minutes, or until tender when poked with a sharp knife. Drain and set aside.

Meanwhile, preheat a broiler or grill to high. Toast the corn ears until nicely browned all over, but not burned (you could even toast them over a naked gas flame). It'll take a good 15–20 minutes to cook the corn. Take off the heat, let cool a little, then slice off the kernels using a sharp knife.

In a small mixing bowl, stir together the mayonnaise, chili powder and jalapeño chili.

Put the potato and corn in a mixing bowl, then stir in the mayo mixture. Add the rest of the ingredients and season with salt and freshly ground black pepper. Mix together gently, then serve.

This is the perfect barbecue salad or lunch. A good sprinkling of fried bacon or chorizo doesn't go astray, and adds a lovely texture.

ICEBERG LETTUCE WITH MINT, RADISH & AVOCADO DRESSING

This salad has an amazing dressing. Also known as a green goddess dressing, it's a simpler version of the one by Alice Waters of Chez Panisse fame in Berkeley, California. **Serves 2–4 sharing**

INGREDIENTS

1 large iceberg lettuce, washed and torn

6 red radishes, trimmed and thinly sliced

1 handful mint, washed and torn

AVOCADO DRESSING

1 large avocado—if you can't get hold of a really large avocado, use 2 regular avocados, or even 3 if small

⅔ cup (150 ml, 5 fl oz) light (single) cream

1 cup (250 ml, 8 fl oz) olive oil

1 shallot, finely chopped

10 anchovy fillets, finely chopped

¼ cup (50 ml, 2 fl oz) chardonnay vinegar (see glossary), or any good vinegar

juice of ½ lemon

1 small handful flat-leaf (Italian) parsley, washed and finely chopped

METHOD

To make the dressing, peel and remove the pit from the avocado, roughly chop the flesh, and place in a mixing bowl with the cream. Blitz together using a handheld immersion blender until smooth. Carefully fold in the other dressing ingredients until incorporated. Season with salt and freshly ground black pepper.

Place the lettuce in a mixing bowl and dress the leaves until they are coated. Any leftover dressing will keep in the fridge for up to 3 days before it starts to discolor.

Add most of the radish and mint to the salad and toss. Place in a serving bowl. Finish with the remaining radish and mint and a wee bit more dressing, then it's ready to go.

NOTE: The super Avocado Dressing has a multitude of uses. For other tasty ideas, see the salad dressing family tree on page 131.

SMOKED TOMATOES WITH BASIL VINAIGRETTE, SHANKLISH & SUMAC

It's true, I love smoked foods—they add a beautiful roundness to dishes, and this recipe reflects this belief. **Serves 4 as a starter or sharing**

INGREDIENTS

4 Smoked Tomatoes (see page 34), each cut into 5 slices

⅔ cup (150 ml, 5 fl oz) Basil Cordial (see page 186)

⅓ cup (80 ml, 2½ fl oz) olive oil

juice of ½ lemon

3 basil leaves, washed and finely shredded

salt to taste

freshly ground black pepper

1 ball mild shanklish (see glossary)

1 teaspoon ground sumac (see glossary)

1 tablespoon chopped flat-leaf (Italian) parsley

METHOD

Arrange the smoked tomatoes on a plate. In a bowl, mix together the cordial, olive oil, lemon juice, and basil. Season with salt and freshly ground black pepper, then drizzle over the tomatoes.

Crumble the shanklish all over the tomatoes and around the plate. Sprinkle with the sumac and parsley and serve.

NOTE: Shankish is a type of cow's milk cheese originally from Syria and Lebanon. It's commonly sold in balls, and has a texture similar to feta.

LATE SUMMER

The abundance of summer fruits and vegetables is well with us. The grill is getting a flogging, and my tan is, well … I'm a little red! I'm actually starting to complain about the heat, but I guess that is my Englishness. The earth is warm, the nighttime air ablaze with the smell of backyard barbecuing, and in certain spots in the garden, I can see where I have neglected to water enough or shade certain plants.

My cucumbers this year are doing brilliantly; I promised myself to plant more this season, as we eat them all so quickly, and it has worked. This said, my attention is drawn to what I should be planting for autumn and the future coming winter. Seedlings are sown for the brassica family; root vegetables are being planned to go into beds. It's a special but careful time in the garden.

CUCUMBERS IN CRÈME FRAÎCHE WITH HERBS

Simply peel your cucumbers, then cut into finger-width lengths. Lightly salt them to help draw out the moisture, then after a few minutes rinse and dry. Now from here you could do all sorts of things. I'd mix them with a good few spoonfuls of crème fraîche or sour cream, and some sea salt and freshly ground black pepper, then finish with lots of finely chopped herbs such as dill, tarragon, and parsley.

SALAD OF PARMA HAM, MELON & RADICCHIO

As a professional cook, you get those flashback moments from kitchens of the past. Time goes so quickly and you work so long that you forget most of the dishes you've cooked, but not the base recipes and skills. This is one of those flashbacks from Restaurant Martin Wishart. We used duck prosciutto then, which I have replaced with Parma ham. **Serves 2–4**

INGREDIENTS

¼ cup (50 g, 2 oz) superfine (caster) sugar

¼ honeydew melon, around ¾ lb (350 g) skinned, seeded, and cut into ¾-inch (2 cm) cubes

¼ musk melon (netted melon, cataluope), around ¾ lb (350 g) skinned, seeded, and cut into ¾-inch (2 cm) cubes

1 small handful baby arugula (rocket) leaves, washed

3 red radicchio leaves, tough white rib removed, then washed and shredded

1 head of frisée (see glossary), yellow part only, washed

2 tablespoons toasted and crushed macadamia nuts

6 thin slices Parma ham (see glossary), prosciutto, or jamón

CREAMY NUTTY LEMON DRESSING

¼ cup (50 ml, 2 fl oz) olive oil

¼ cup (50 ml, 2 fl oz) hazelnut oil

¼ cup (50 ml, 2 fl oz) walnut oil

juice of ½ lemon

¼ cup (50 ml, 2 fl oz) sherry vinegar

1 teaspoon salt

5 good turns of black pepper

¼ cup (50 ml, 2 fl oz) light (single) cream

METHOD

To make the dressing, put the oils, lemon juice, vinegar, salt, and pepper in a bowl. Whisk together and set aside.

Heat a large frying pan over medium heat and add the sugar. Let the sugar dissolve, and when it turns to a light caramel color, throw in all the melon and stir until the melon starts to warm. Cook to caramelize one side of the melon pieces. Take off the heat, remove the melon from the pan, and keep warm.

Add the dressing to the pan and leave to cook until reduced to one-third. Now add the cream and whisk until fully combined. Take the dressing off the heat, but keep it warm.

Have the salad leaves in a mixing bowl and dress with some of the warm dressing. Gently toss in the warm melon pieces, then arrange on your platter or serving plates.

Layer the ham over the top and sprinkle with the macadamias. Drizzle with a little more dressing and serve.

FRIED GREEN TOMATOES WITH FIG ANCHOÏADE

An exquisite way to use two late summer/early autumn "fruits." In the dark of night, you may just catch me walking the back streets of Melbourne, "borrowing" figs and other fruits from overhanging trees … Green tomatoes are simply delicious fried like this—a great way to use up those never-ripening gems. This dish also goes well with baked ham wedges or some pan-fried calamari. **Serves 4**

INGREDIENTS

3 large green tomatoes

salt to sprinkle

1 cup (150 g, 5½ oz) quick-cooking polenta

2 teaspoons confectioners' (icing) sugar, sifted

½ teaspoon finely ground black pepper

¾ cup (180 ml, 6 fl oz) olive oil

1 small handful small-leaf green mustard cress or mizuna leaves, washed

FIG ANCHOÏADE

3 really ripe figs, chopped

1 piquillo pepper (see glossary), or preserved or roasted bell pepper, chopped

4 anchovy fillets, chopped

2 garlic cloves, chopped

12 blanched almonds, chopped

1 teaspoon fennel seeds

⅔ cup (150 ml, 5 fl oz) olive oil

juice of ½ lemon

1 small handful flat-leaf (Italian) parsley leaves, washed and chopped

2 teaspoons orange flower water (see glossary)

salt to taste

freshly ground black pepper

METHOD

Start by making the Fig Anchoïade. Place the figs, piquillo pepper, anchovies, garlic, almonds, fennel seeds, and olive oil in a blender and blitz until smooth. Scoop the mixture into a bowl, then slowly fold in the lemon juice, parsley, and orange flower water. Season with salt and freshly ground black pepper and set aside.

Slice the tops and bottoms off the tomatoes, then cut each tomato into four slices. Lightly sprinkle with salt and leave to sit for 3 minutes. (I salt the tomatoes to draw out a little moisture and to soften them.) Place the slices on a tea towel (dish towel) and pat dry.

Mix together the polenta, confectioners' sugar, and black pepper. Pat each tomato slice into the polenta mixture, coating them on each side. Place on a plate, ready to fry.

Preheat the oven to 375ºF (190ºC, Gas 5). Heat a large frying pan over medium heat and add half the olive oil (we'll do the frying in a few stages). Without crowding the pan too much and adding more oil as needed, fry the tomatoes on both sides for a couple of minutes, or until golden, placing each batch on a metal tray lined with paper towels and heating through in the oven for 4 minutes until cooked.

Once out of the oven, arrange the tomato slices on a plate. Spoon the fig anchoïade over and sprinkle with the mustard leaves. Serve warm.

NOTE: You can use your Fig Anchoïade to dress up many different dishes; see the salad dressing family tree on page 131.

SUMMER

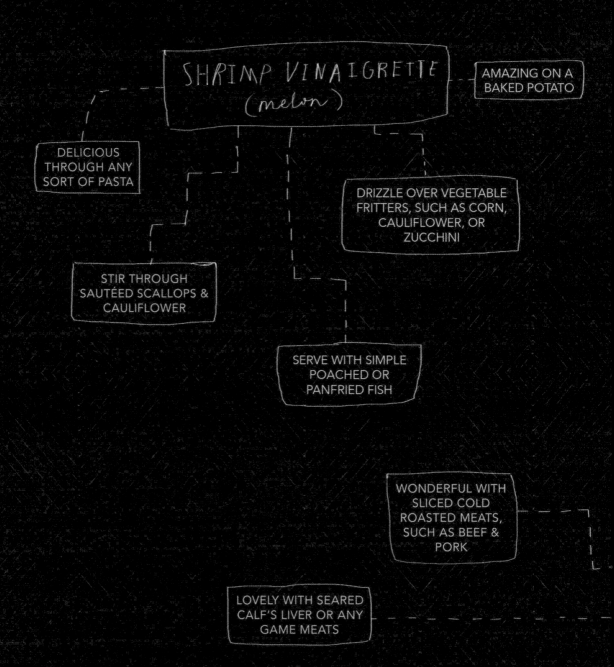

SHRIMP VINAIGRETTE
(melon)

AMAZING ON A BAKED POTATO

DELICIOUS THROUGH ANY SORT OF PASTA

DRIZZLE OVER VEGETABLE FRITTERS, SUCH AS CORN, CAULIFLOWER, OR ZUCCHINI

STIR THROUGH SAUTÉED SCALLOPS & CAULIFLOWER

SERVE WITH SIMPLE POACHED OR PANFRIED FISH

WONDERFUL WITH SLICED COLD ROASTED MEATS, SUCH AS BEEF & PORK

LOVELY WITH SEARED CALF'S LIVER OR ANY GAME MEATS

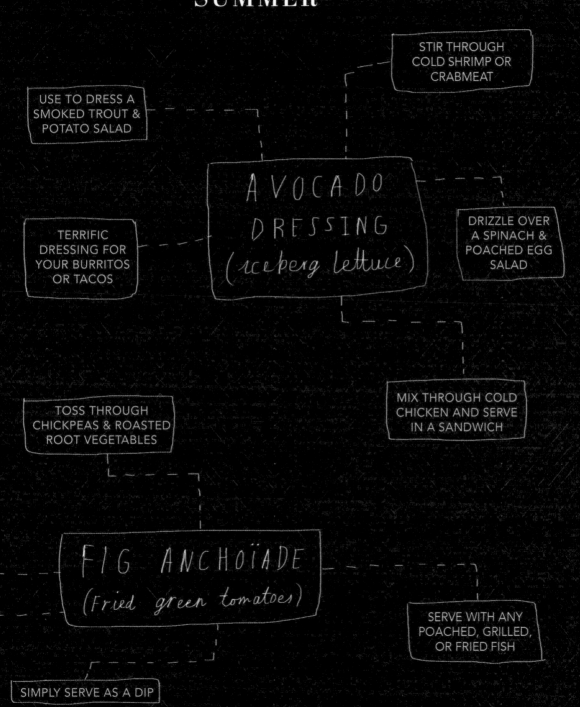

SALAD DRESSING FAMILY TREE
SUMMER

STIR THROUGH
COLD SHRIMP OR
CRABMEAT

USE TO DRESS A
SMOKED TROUT &
POTATO SALAD

AVOCADO
DRESSING
(iceberg lettuce)

TERRIFIC
DRESSING FOR
YOUR BURRITOS
OR TACOS

DRIZZLE OVER
A SPINACH &
POACHED EGG
SALAD

MIX THROUGH COLD
CHICKEN AND SERVE
IN A SANDWICH

TOSS THROUGH
CHICKPEAS & ROASTED
ROOT VEGETABLES

FIG ANCHOÏADE
(Fried green tomatoes)

SERVE WITH ANY
POACHED, GRILLED,
OR FRIED FISH

SIMPLY SERVE AS A DIP

PEACHES WITH GRATED MACADAMIA & SQUASHED BLUEBERRIES

There is nothing more beautiful than a simple peach. Blanch and peel, you ask? You don't have to, it's up to you, but I think it's worth it. The vinegar brings out the flavor in the whole dish, but especially the amazing blueberries I get from my friend Mal, from Moondarra Blueberries. **Serves 4**

INGREDIENTS

4 ripe yellow peaches

½ cup (100 g, 4 oz) crème fraîche or mascarpone

1 teaspoon vanilla paste (I use Heilala)

1 cup plus 2 tablespoons (250 g, 9 oz) fresh blueberries

1 tablespoon cabernet vinegar, or a really good red wine vinegar

2 teaspoons superfine (caster) sugar

3 macadamia nuts

METHOD

Place a pot of water on to boil.

Using a sharp knife, score the base of the peaches with a cross. Place them into the boiling water and leave for 10–20 seconds, until the skin starts to come away. Remove the peaches with a slotted spoon and immediately run under cold water. Peel off the skin and cut each peach in half, carefully removing the pit. Place two peach halves in each serving dish.

Mix together the crème fraîche and vanilla paste and spoon over the peaches.

In another mixing bowl, crush the blueberries using your hands, then mix in the vinegar and sugar. Divide among your serving dishes.

Using a microplane, grate the macadamia nuts over it all and enjoy.

BLACKBERRY & BAY LEAF CORDIAL

BLACK BERRY & BAY LEAF CORDIAL
INGREDIENTS
2 lb 3 oz (1 kg) blackberries thoroughly washed & drained
2 generous cups (500 g) sugar
2 fresh bay leaves
1 tablespoon (15 g, ½ oz) citric acid (see glossary)

I love blackberry picking in the country, but make sure if you are going that you ask permission … and make sure they haven't sprayed any nasty chemicals onto the plants, as blackberry is considered a weed in most places.

Makes about 6⅓ cups (1.5 liters)

METHOD

Place the blackberries in a blender and blitz until smooth. Transfer to a large pot, then add the rest of the ingredients and 2 cups (500 ml, 17 fl oz) water. Bring to a boil over medium heat, scooping off any impurities using a spoon. Reduce the heat and simmer for 15 minutes.

Strain through a sieve, then pour into sterilized jars and seal.

Keep in a cool dark place for up to 6 months. Once opened, store in the fridge for up to 8 weeks.

STRAWBERRY, BLACK PEPPER & CUCUMBER CORDIAL

Whether you have kids or not, strawberry picking is so much fun. There should be a national holiday just to go strawberry picking at a farm for the day. Strawberry, cucumber, and black pepper are a classic match and lovely in a cordial.

You could also place fresh borage flowers into the bottles with the cordial, like we do. **Makes 7¼ cups (1¾ liters)**

METHOD

Put your strawberries and cucumbers into a blender and purée. Transfer to a large pot, then stir in the sugar, apple juice, citric acid, pepper, and 2 cups (500 ml, 17 fl oz) water.

Bring to a boil over medium heat, then ladle off and discard any impurities that rise to the surface. Reduce the heat and simmer on low for 10 minutes.

Strain through a sieve, then pour into sterilized bottles and seal.

Keep in a cool dark place for up to 6 months. Once opened, store in the fridge for up to 8 weeks.

STRAWBERRY, BLACK PEPPER & CUCUMBER CORDIAL

INGREDIENTS

1¾ lb (750g) strawberries washed & tops removed

2 lb 3 oz (1 kg) lebanese cucumbers, peeled

4 cups (750g, 2 lb 11 oz) sugar

1 cup (250ml, 8 fl oz) apple juice

1 tablespoon (15g, ½ oz) citric acid (see glossary)

1½ teaspoons freshly ground black pepper

AUTUMN

AUTUMN

FOR ME, MORE THAN ANY OTHER SEASON, AUTUMN IS BROKEN INTO TWO HALVES: EARLY AND LATE.

Early autumn is taking advantage of the last of the summer bounty. There is the last of the tomatoes, zucchini, and corn coming through in the garden. It is all about getting the most out of the days, while it is still light in the afternoons, before the chill of winter descends, before the days get shorter and the sunlight diminishes.

Autumn mornings are amazing—crisp, clean, and cold—and the nights are clear and full of stars. I love to get out and forage and fish before it gets too cold. This is the season of mushrooms and mushrooming. Of earthy scents and flavors. There are endless goodies that we can now get all year round which used to be "seasonal," but if you really want to enjoy produce at its peak, indulge yourself by going to your local farmers' market in autumn and getting a selection of wild mushrooms from around your area. Cook them down in a pan with a bit of butter, seasoning, and some soft herbs … what a start to the day on toast!

In Victoria, autumn is the best time to eat pears and apples, and it is also the season for hunting and eating game. Game is considered to be any animal that is hunted for food and not normally domesticated. In Australia, this can include deer, duck, rabbit … and even crocodile, emu, and kangaroo! In Ol' Blighty it also includes more traditional birds such as grouse, pheasant, quail, and partridge. (In my head, I just got this image of Bugs Bunny and Daffy Duck arguing over whether it is "duck season" or "wabbit season" and Elmer Fudd trying to shoot them both!)

Late autumn brings with it a certain moodiness. The nights become longer, and the cold settles in. There is such rich color all around—all the gorgeous, varied shades of different yellows, reds, and oranges when the leaves turn on the trees before they fall to the ground. Which is why, of course, Americans refer to this season as "fall." Interestingly, autumn was called "fall" in England too, and the pilgrims took this word with them to the New World. The word fell out of favor and use in Britain, but remained in America.

Autumn was traditionally the season for preserving meats, to take full advantage of winter's drop in temperature, ensuring the meat wouldn't spoil when hung out. I have such fond memories of being invited by my friends, Jo and Arnie Pizzini, to their home in the glorious King Valley in northeast Victoria to help with their annual salami and sausage making. I love that in this age we live in—in which everything is so readily available—there are communities who still delight in the custom and art of making and enjoying their own cured meats. It is a tradition that goes back centuries in so many cultures around the world, and I hope that it will continue for centuries to come. It is such a wonderful way to engage people in the food that they are consuming of communing with nature and the seasons.

Autumn is the time to conserve as much of summer's bounty as we can, including olives and grapes. Autumn is the season of winemaking and oil production. There are regions of Italy, such as Umbria, for example, which are renowned for their autumn oil and winemaking, practices that have been going on in nearly the same fashion (give or take some modern technology) for millennia. The Roman Empire was built on the skills of the Italian vintners and olive farmers being able to make the most of the year's harvest in autumn and preserving it in earthenware pots called amphora that could be transported to the far reaches of the Empire, to feed and "water" the troops. Archaeological sites all around the United Kingdom are littered with their remnants.

We forget today, in the golden age of the supermarket, that once upon a time, and not too many centuries ago either, this was life and death stuff. Autumn was the harvest period (prior to the fifteenth century, the season was actually called "harvest"), and food needed to be preserved and stored properly so that there was enough to sustain farmers and their families or communities throughout the long winter period.

In the northern hemisphere, particularly America, autumn is associated with the holidays of Halloween and particularly Thanksgiving—where the pilgrims gave thanks for the fact that the Native Americans shared their autumn harvest, saving the Founding Fathers from starving to death after their own crops failed.

Back home in the United Kingdom, nearly every little town or village has its own harvest festivals. I have fond memories of using the freshly milled wheat, oats, and barley to make bread and biscuits when I was a lad at school as part of the celebrations. Britons have been celebrating the end of the harvest since pagan times, and while it is a lovely practice even now, centuries ago it was central to the role of religion in everyday life. The festival was to thank God for the bounty that He had provided, and was a reminder to Christians to share with those less fortunate. Produce of the season is fundamental to these special days. I mean, what would Thanksgiving be without pumpkin pie or Halloween without the carved pumpkin jack-o-lantern?

Getting back closer to home, autumn is a great time to enrich your garden with a good feed. It has given so much of its nutrients to the summer plants, and it really needs to be replenished. It will benefit from a good mulching too.

Start putting your brassicas in, ready for winter. Now is the time to plant out carrots (my favorites) and beets too.

Also take advantage of the fact that the fabales family (which includes peas, beans, chickpeas, and lentils) are in season twice throughout the year—in autumn and spring. They pack a natural nitrogen punch, and are fantastic for releasing nutrients back to the soil after the abundant summer produce has depleted it. This will get your soil back into shape to support the slow-growing brassicas over winter.

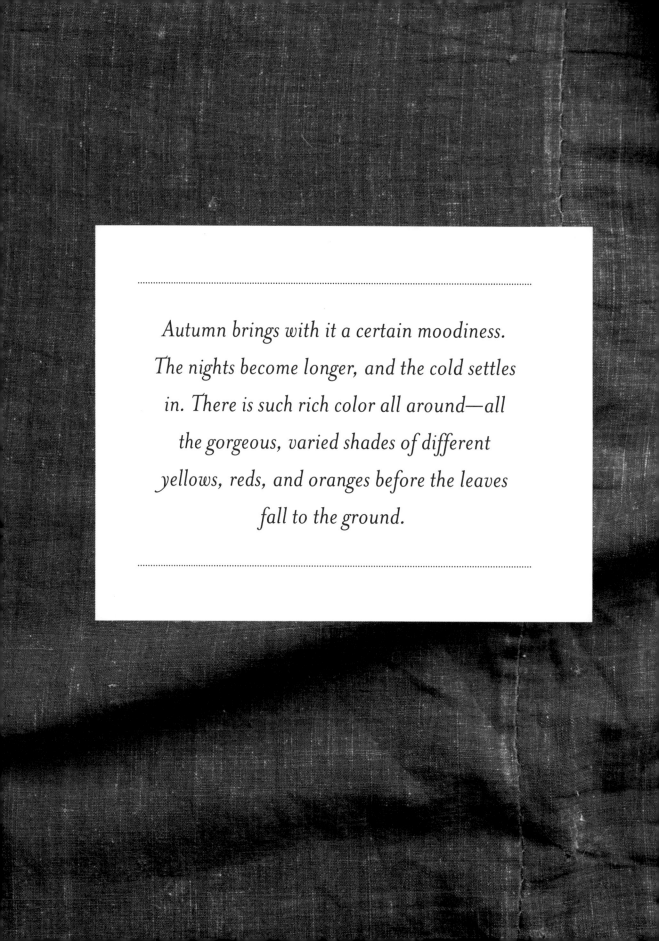

Autumn brings with it a certain moodiness. The nights become longer, and the cold settles in. There is such rich color all around—all the gorgeous, varied shades of different yellows, reds, and oranges before the leaves fall to the ground.

BROWN RICE & FETA SALAD WITH HOT 'N' SOUR DRESSING

I used to hate brown rice—childhood memories of canned tuna and frozen corn, uck!—until a trip to New South Wales, where I met the McConnell family, who are amazing biodynamic growers. They cooked lunch for me and I ate this rice for the first time. The nutty complexity of it is divine. So good simply boiled, but in this salad, excellent. **Serves 4**

INGREDIENTS

2 cups (300 g, 11 oz) biodynamic brown koshi rice (see glossary), or similar alternative

½ cup (100 g, 4 oz) French green lentils

3½ oz (100 g) soft Danish-style feta

2 tablespoons (20 ml, 1 fl oz) milk

2 tablespoons chopped almonds

2 tablespoons chopped dried apricots

4 dried pears, chopped

6 sorrel leaves (see glossary), washed and finely shredded

salt to taste

freshly ground black pepper

1 tablespoon Dukkah (see page 30)

1 tablespoon pepitas (pumpkin seeds)

HOT 'N' SOUR DRESSING

6 hot long green pickled chilies (from a jar), finely chopped

3 shallots, sliced

1 cup (125 g, 4 oz) blonde sultanas (see glossary), or other good sultanas (golden raisins)

½ cup (100 ml, 4 fl oz) chardonnay vinegar (see glossary)

1 cup (250 ml, 8 fl oz) olive oil

4 tablespoons salted capers, rinsed

1 tablespoon superfine (caster) sugar

METHOD

This may seem like a lot of work for a salad, but it's really easy, trust me.

Rinse the rice in cold water first, then place in an 8-cup (2 liter) pot and add 6 cups (1.5 liters) of cold water. Bring to a boil, then reduce the heat and simmer for 20 minutes. Test the rice and when it is cooked, strain and set aside.

Meanwhile, put the lentils in a different pot with 4 cups (1 liter) of cold water. Bring to a boil, then reduce the heat and simmer for 20–25 minutes, or until just tender. Strain and mix with the rice.

For the dressing, place all the ingredients in a small saucepan, stir together, warm a little over low heat and it's ready to go.

Mix the feta and milk together to moisten the cheese a little.

Now add the almonds, apricots, pears, and sorrel to the rice and lentils. Add a good few tablespoons of the dressing and gently combine, making sure you get a bit of everything from the dressing. Add more dressing if needed to coat all the grains, and season with salt and freshly ground black pepper. This recipe makes a fair bit of dressing, but whatever you don't use will keep in the fridge in a clean airtight jar for months.

Place half the salad into your serving bowls. Dollop half the feta over the top, then add the remaining salad. Finish with the last of the feta, then sprinkle with the dukkah and pepitas.

NOTE: See the salad dressing family tree on page 182 for other delicious ways to use the Hot 'n' Sour Dressing.

SMASHED FIGS WITH BLUE CHEESE, WALNUTS & WHITE BALSAMIC

I wish I'd been introduced to figs a lot earlier in my life. Picking them straight from the tree, sun warmed, is just sublime. Where I live there are hundreds of fig trees overhanging onto footpaths and back alleyways, so it would be rude not to help myself to some on the way home. **Serves 2 sharing**

INGREDIENTS

5 ripe figs, cut in half

1¾ oz (50 g) blue cheese; I like to use gorgonzola for this dish

10 walnuts, toasted and chopped

8 basil leaves, washed and torn

2 tablespoons (20 ml, 1 fl oz) white balsamic vinegar (see glossary), or regular balsamic vinegar, if not available

2 tablespoons (20 ml, 1 fl oz) good olive oil

1 tablespoon pepitas (pumpkin seeds), toasted

good pinch of salt

a few turns of white pepper

2 slices bread, toasted

METHOD

Take two sheets of parchment paper, each about 12 inches (30 cm) long. On one sheet place the figs, flesh side down, then cover with the other piece of baking paper. Now gently smash the figs using your fingers until they are flat. Once smashed, take off the top layer of paper, leaving the figs on the bottom sheet.

Turn the bottom sheet of paper upside down onto a plate, then gently remove the paper. Now crumble the cheese over the figs, then scatter with the walnuts and basil.

Drizzle the vinegar and olive oil all over, then sprinkle with the pepitas, salt, and pepper. Serve with toasted bread on the side.

EARLY AUTUMN

I get easily confused in the garden in early autumn. The apples, pears, and figs are ready—such a delight to cook with and eat raw—but I'm starting to find the summer vegetables and fruits a little tiresome. I've gorged myself on them so much, and the plants themselves are starting to look a little tired. I'm still waiting for some eggplants to get bigger and the bell peppers to turn a vibrant red.

The kitchen is full of just harvested goods to preserve for a later time; I'm making and bottling my tomato sugo and chutneys of all kinds. My beans, peas, and fava beans are coming on brilliantly, as is my spinach, kale, and Swiss chard.

I'm loving the last of the berries—fighting my children, the Mrs. and our crazy dog, Quincy, as to who gets to pick and eat the strawberries straight from the plant. And just enjoying the last of my raspberries and blackberries before the end of the warmer weather …

RECIPE:

SPINACH, GORGONZOLA & CRUSHED RASPBERRIES

I do love a good simple baby spinach leaf salad. When the leaves get too big, I don't eat them raw, but make a pie or sauté them with a little garlic. However the small leaves make a wonderful leaf salad. So, wash and dry a good few handfuls of baby spinach, then place in a bowl. To this add some crumbled blue cheese—I prefer a gorgonzola—then toast some walnuts and toss them through. In a separate bowl take a good cup of raspberries and smash them up a little using your fingers or a fork. Add sea salt, freshly ground black pepper, and a splash of red wine vinegar, and mix through the salad with a little olive oil.

SALAD OF ENDIVE, GRAPES, WALNUTS & QUAIL

A good friend of mine, Riccardo Momesso, took me quail shooting once. Afterwards we sat on a hill overlooking the country, eating grilled, just shot quail. An amazing surreal day, but it hit home just how great simple food can be. This is one of those dishes. **Serves 2 as a main, or 4 as a starter**

INGREDIENTS

4 jumbo or extra-large quails, butterflied

⅔ cup (150 ml, 5 fl oz) canola oil (non-GMO)

⅓ cup (80 ml, 2½ fl oz) verjuice (see glossary)

1 teaspoon salt

½ teaspoon ground cumin

½ teaspoon ground sumac (see glossary)

2 tablespoons walnuts

1 white/yellow Belgian endive (witlof or chicory), leaves separated and washed

1 small handful watercress, leaves picked and washed

20 seedless grapes, cut in half

juice of ½ lemon

⅓ cup (80 ml, 2½ fl oz) olive oil

salt to taste

freshly ground black pepper

METHOD

Marinate the quails in the canola oil, verjuice, salt, and spices for at least 30 minutes—it's really good if you can marinate the quails one or two days before.

When you're ready to cook, heat a broiler or grill to high. Toast the walnuts in a small cast-iron pan under the broiler or on the grill for 3–4 minutes, or until fragrant. Set aside.

Cook the quails, bone side down, for 7–9 minutes, depending on their size. Flip them over onto the skin side, then turn the heat down to medium. Cook for 5 minutes, then the quails should be ready. Check by piercing the thickest part of the thigh with a skewer; the juices should run clear.

In a mixing bowl, toss the endive, watercress, grapes, lemon juice, and olive oil with some salt and freshly ground black pepper.

Once the quails are cooked, lay them on your serving plates and pile the salad alongside, scattering the walnuts over to finish.

CRAB, SAMPHIRE & MUSTARD ON TOAST

I think I first tasted something like this when vacationing on the east coast of England when I was little, but this tasty dish has come and gone on my menus for a while now. Samphire? Just try it, it rocks!

Some other variations are to add caviar or salmon roe instead of the dried mullet at the end or to whip avocado with a little fromage blanc and dollop on top. But don't feel you have to use the dried mullet and the Parmesan—it's just as delicious without. You should use the best crabmeat you can find.

Serves 2 as a plated starter, or 4 sharing

INGREDIENTS

7 oz (200 g) cooked crabmeat

20 samphire sprigs (see glossary), picked and washed

1 large red mustard leaf (see glossary), washed and torn

1 handful baby spinach leaves, washed

2 slices cornbread, toasted and cut into long rectangles

a few turns of white pepper

1 oz (25 g) Parmesan

¾ oz (20 g) piece of dried mullet or tuna roe (bottarga) (see glossary)

2 tablespoons (20 ml, 1 fl oz) balsamic vinegar

CREAMY MUSTARD DRESSING

½ cup (100 ml, 4 fl oz) heavy (thick, double) cream

¼ cup (50 g, 2 oz) dijon mustard

2 tablespoons (20 ml, 1 fl oz) chardonnay vinegar (see glossary)

pinch of sugar

2 pinches of salt

METHOD

Preheat the oven to 325°F (170°C, Gas 3).

To make the dressing, whisk together the cream, mustard, vinegar, sugar, and salt.

In an ovenproof bowl, place the crabmeat, samphire, mustard leaf, and baby spinach. Dress the mixture with the dressing to coat the leaves, then place in the oven for 1–2 minutes—just long enough to break the leaves a little. Take out of the oven and mix gently.

Lay the cornbread on serving plates, then randomly spoon the crab mixture all around. Finish with some turns of white pepper, then microplane the Parmesan and bottarga over. Drizzle with the vinegar and serve warm.

NOTE: Samphire is also called sea pickle. It is salty and a little crunchy. You can substitute capers or another pickled sea vegetable.

SALAD OF CLAMS, POTATO, SORREL & SOUR CREAM

The beginning of autumn says hello to wonderful new potatoes. These, mixed with clams that have been feasting over the summer, make for a sublime dish. Add a little zing of sorrel, a slurp of sour cream, and a hint of white pepper, and it's simply delicious. **Serves 4**

INGREDIENTS

2 lb 3 oz (1 kg) large hardshell clams

2 lb 3 oz (1 kg) small new potatoes

¼ cup (60 g, 2 oz) sour cream

3 cornichons (see glossary), roughly chopped

2 sorrel leaves (see glossary), washed and torn

a good few turns of white pepper

salt to taste

METHOD

Place a large pot on the stove, pop the lid on and place on high heat for 2 minutes. Add the clams and ½ cup (100 ml, 4 fl oz) water to the pot. Put the lid back on and cook the clams for 3–5 minutes, shaking all the time, until all the clams have opened. Strain into a colander, reserving the juices. Pick the clams from the shells straight away and set aside.

Meanwhile, peel the potatoes and cut them, if needed, into the size of a wine screwcap. Place in a pot filled with water and bring to a boil. Turn the heat down to a gentle simmer and cook for 10–12 minutes, or until just tender. Drain and set aside.

Wash out that pot and add ½ cup (100 ml, 4 fl oz) of the reserved clam liquid. Bring to a boil, allow the liquid to reduce by half, then whisk in the sour cream.

Pour the sour cream dressing over the cooked potatoes and toss gently. Mix in the clams, cornichons, and sorrel.

Place in a serving bowl, then add the white pepper. Taste and add a pinch of salt if you like.

Perfect with a glass of white wine and some crusty bread.

PURPLE CONGO POTATOES, SUNCHOKES & ANCHOVY DRESSING

This is one of those dishes that makes you proud. It started off as something that wasn't quite right, but the whole kitchen team worked on it to make it beautiful. Sunchokes (or Jerusalem artichokes, as most people call them) didn't make it into my first book, so here they are. **Serves 2**

INGREDIENTS

2 large purple potatoes, or other boiling potatoes, washed

1 lb 2 oz (500 g) sunchokes (Jerusalem artichokes)

2 tablespoons (20 ml, 1 fl oz) light (pouring, single) cream

½ cup (100 ml, 4 fl oz) olive oil

2 tablespoons salted capers, rinsed

2 free-range eggs, hard-boiled for 8 minutes, then peeled and grated

4 cups (1 liter) canola oil (non-GMO)

1 tablespoon rice flour

1 large red mustard leaf (see glossary), washed and cut into thin strips

ANCHOVY & DIJON DRESSING

2 oz (50 g) anchovy fillets

¼ teaspoon dijon mustard

splash of chardonnay vinegar (see glossary)

2 cups (500 ml, 17 fl oz) light (pouring, single) cream

METHOD

Preheat the oven to 375°F (190°C, Gas 5). Cut each potato in half, keeping the skin on, then place in a pot of water. Bring to a boil and cook for 18–22 minutes, or until tender. Once cooked, remove the potatoes from the water and leave to cool to room temperature. Peel the potatoes, reserving the peels. Thickly slice the potatoes.

Meanwhile, peel half the sunchokes, reserving the peels with the potato peels. Place the peeled sunchokes in a pot with just enough water to cover. Bring to a boil, then reduce the heat and simmer for 6–9 minutes, or until fully cooked. Drain, place in a blender, and purée until smooth, adding the cream and half of the olive oil.

Roughly chop the remaining sunchokes. Spread on a baking tray, drizzle with the remaining olive oil, and bake for 12–15 minutes, or until tender.

To make the dressing, get a mortar and pestle and grind together the anchovies and mustard to make a fine paste. Add the vinegar to thin out the mixture, then whisk in the cream.

In a deep-sided pot, heat the canola oil to 350°F (180°C) on a cooking thermometer. Quickly fry the capers until golden and crispy, then remove with a slotted spoon and drain on paper towels.

Lightly dust the potato and sunchoke peels with the rice flour, then fry in the hot oil until crisp, about 2 minutes. Remove with a slotted spoon and drain on paper towels—you just made potato and sunchoke crisps!

Add the cooked potatoes and sunchokes to a mixing bowl. Drizzle with a little of the dressing (about 4 tablespoons) to coat. Add half the capers and half the grated egg, then toss gently. Spoon the sunchoke purée around your serving plates, then pile the salad on top. Finish with the last of the capers and egg, the mustard leaf, and fried crisps.

NOTE: For other tasty uses for your Anchovy Dressing, see the salad dressing family tree on page 183.

MID-AUTUMN

What an amazing time in the garden. My pumpkins and watermelons have finally colored up, ready for picking and tidying up the long vines taking up so much of the garden. The basil is crazy, and it is now time to harvest and make my most loathed dressing, loved so much by my family—pesto!

Out in the countryside it's mushroom season, rediscovering our secret spots in the hunt for the morels, hen of the woods, and black trumpet. Driving in and around the areas where we hunt for mushrooms, the nuts are falling from the trees: chestnuts, walnuts, almonds, hazelnuts. It's a marvellous time, cold mornings foraging and gathering wild foods. I love it.

My neighbors' trees are full of figs and quinces now, and the first of the pomegranates are ready. It's time for me to "help" harvest my neighbors' and the council's trees that are overhanging onto the streets, laneways, and roads. I do hope they thank me soon …

I HATE PESTO SALAD

The kids and the boss love pesto. Me, I think it's the pine nuts mixed with the basil that I just can't stomach. That said, I make buckets of pesto at this time of year, harvesting the last of the basil, freezing pesto ready to be thawed at a later stage. My basic rule of thumb for pesto is two big handfuls of basil, 1 tablespoon toasted pine nuts, 2 tablespoons grated parmesan, the grated zest and juice of half a lemon, some sea salt, freshly ground black pepper, enough olive oil to just cover it all, then blend to a smooth paste. In our house it's generally for lunch—cold, leftover thick-shaped pasta with blanched green beans and extra parmesan over the top.

Me, I cover it in a chilli sauce, which makes it okay, but we also use it on boiled potatoes or a roasted vegetable salad, such as squash, parsnip, carrot, and sweet potato. Toss some shaved fennel through it, dress with pesto … and hey presto! (Sorry about that line.)

Once upon a time, before the golden age of the supermarket, autumn was the harvest period—life and death stuff. Food needed to be preserved and stored properly to sustain people throughout the long, lean winter ahead.

BABY RED BEETS COOKED IN CRANBERRY JUICE WITH RICOTTA, CUMIN & DILL

I have no problem saying, "I love you, beet!" We cook them in cranberry juice to add to the natural sweetness of the beets, then finish them over a grill to add a smoky caramelized flavor.
Serves 2–4 sharing

INGREDIENTS

14–18 baby red beets, no bigger than about 1¼ inch (3 cm)

4 cups (1 liter, 34 fl oz) cranberry juice

½ cup (100 ml, 4 fl oz) red wine vinegar

2 tablespoons (20 ml, 1 fl oz) olive oil

1 teaspoon ground cumin

1 tablespoon honey

4 oz (100 g) ricotta

2 teaspoons chopped dill

METHOD

Give the beets a really good scrub. Trim the tops and keep these for a nice salad later. Put the beets in a pot, along with the cranberry juice and vinegar. Bring to a boil, reduce the heat to a simmer, and cook for 22–26 minutes, or until you can insert a small sharp knife through the beets easily. Strain the cranberry juice mixture into a clean saucepan and reserve.

Now peel the beets—while still hot, baby!—by rubbing them between sheets of paper towel, discarding the skins. Set the beets aside.

Cook the reserved cranberry juice mixture over a medium heat, until it has reduced to a balsamic glaze consistency, ½ cup (100 ml, 4 fl oz). Set aside.

Place a large frying pan over high heat. Add the olive oil, then pan-fry the beets for 3–4 minutes, or until browned all over. Add the cumin and toast for a further 1 minute, then add the honey and the glazed cranberry juice mixture. Cook for a further 3 minutes, then take off the heat.

Spoon the beets into a bowl. Drizzle with half the cooking liquid, which makes a wonderful dressing. Dollop the ricotta all over and sprinkle with the dill. Enjoy warm.

SALAD OF GOLDEN BEETS, PICKLED PLUM, PANCETTA & MAPLE SYRUP

This recipe is one of the many beautiful lunchtime specials we've had at Pope Joan from my executive chef, Jason Newton. He has a beautiful way with food that leaves you inspired and wanting more. We add smoked eel to this salad, but since it's not everybody's cup of tea, we have left it out here. Go on, add it back … **Serves 4 as a starter or sharing**

INGREDIENTS

12–14 baby golden beets, scrubbed and trimmed

4 teaspoons (50 g, 1¾ oz) superfine (caster) sugar

⅓ cup (80 ml, 2½ fl oz) apple cider vinegar

2 star anise

10 black peppercorns

3 firm Japanese or any large plums, pits removed, cut into 6 wedges

½ cup (100 g, 4 oz) Smoked Yogurt (see page 35) or plain yogurt

1 small handful mâche (see glossary), trimmed

2 small watermelon radishes, or regular radishes

¼ cup (25 g, 1 oz) walnuts, toasted and crushed

PANCETTA, ORANGE & MAPLE DRESSING

2 tablespoons (20 ml, 1 fl oz) olive oil

4 oz (100 g) thin slices pancetta or bacon

2 shallots, diced

1 garlic clove, diced

1 teaspoon horseradish paste

juice of 1 orange

2 tablespoons (20 ml, 1 fl oz) sherry vinegar

½ cup (100 ml, 4 fl oz) maple syrup

¾ cup plus 2 tablespoons (200 ml, 7 fl oz) olive oil

METHOD

Place beets in a large pot with the sugar, cider vinegar, star anise, and peppercorns. Pour in enough cold water to cover the beets. Bring to a boil, then reduce the heat and simmer for 22–26 minutes, or until cooked through. Take off the heat to cool.

Strain the beets' pickling liquid into another pot, then let it bubble away until reduced by half.

Meanwhile, peel the cooled beets by rubbing each one between your fingers. Discard the peels. Slice the beets into a bowl, then pour the reduced pickling liquid over them, reserving ½ cup (100 ml, 4 fl oz).

To make the dressing, take a frying pan and heat 2 tablespoons (30 ml, 1 fl oz) of the olive oil over medium heat. Add the pancetta and cook for 2–4 minutes, then add the shallot and garlic and cook, without allowing them to color. Add the horseradish paste, orange juice, sherry vinegar, and maple syrup and reduce the mixture by half, skimming off any impurities that rise to the surface. Take off the heat and whisk in the remaining olive oil.

Broil the plum wedges under medium heat for 1–2 minutes on each side. Place in a bowl with the reserved pickling liquid.

To serve, spread the yogurt on a serving plate like a mad artist (Jason's words). Remove the beets from the pickling liquid and warm over medium heat or in the oven before placing onto the plate.

Remove the plums from the pickling liquid and add to the beets with some mâche and radish, and gently build the salad. Spoon on generous amounts of dressing and finish with the walnuts.

FAVA BEAN, MINT, PARSLEY & POMEGRANATE FATTOUSH

I have this love affair with Arabic flavors; it all started when I moved to Melbourne and discovered them. There is something magical about the flavors, texture, ease, and yet complexity to the dishes—none more so than a fattoush, seasonally changing with whatever is around. **Serves 2–4 sharing**

INGREDIENTS

1 large pita bread

olive oil, for brushing and drizzling

½ teaspoon ground cumin

1 cup (175 g, 6 oz) shelled fresh fava (broad) beans

1 large handful mint, washed and roughly chopped

1 large handful flat-leaf (Italian) parsley, washed and roughly chopped

1 small red onion, thinly sliced

4 radishes, thinly sliced

seeds of 1 pomegranate

juice of 1 lemon

good pinch of ground sumac (see glossary)

METHOD

Preheat the oven to 375°F (190°C, Gas 5). Dampen the pita bread; this will help to "steam bake" the bread, keeping it a little moist, but crispy on the outside. Place on a baking tray, then into the oven, and bake for 4–5 minutes on each side, or until starting to go a little crisp. Take out of the oven and brush with some olive oil, then sprinkle the cumin over. Once cool, tear into small pieces.

Meanwhile, bring a saucepan of water to a boil. Add the fava beans and cook for 2 minutes. Remove using a slotted spoon and refresh under cold water. When the beans are cool enough to handle, gently squeeze them out of their leathery skins.

Roughly chop the fava beans and place in a mixing bowl. Add the mint, parsley, onion, radish, and pomegranate seeds and toss gently to combine. Add the lemon juice, then drizzle on enough olive oil to coat. Add the toasted pita pieces and the sumac, toss again, and serve.

The fattoush also goes nicely with a little yogurt on the side.

SALAD OF KALE, CHEDDAR & FRIED EGG

Kale is such an easy and friendly thing to grow in the garden, and is now known as a superfood. Whatever, it's just delicious. **Serves 2**

INGREDIENTS

¾ lb 2 oz (400 g) kale or fresh spinach

¼ cup (50 ml, 2 fl oz) canola oil (non-GMO)

2 large free-range eggs

almonds

1 small handful flat-leaf (Italian) parsley, washed and chopped

salt to taste

freshly ground black pepper

finely grated Parmesan, for sprinkling

CHEDDAR & ALMOND DRESSING

¼ cup (50 ml, 2 fl oz) milk

4 oz (100 g) Cheddar, grated

½ teaspoon chardonnay vinegar (see glossary)

½ teaspoon butter

1 teaspoon cornstarch (cornflour)

1 tablespoon chopped almonds

METHOD

Wash and dry the kale, but do not shake off all the excess water. Cut the leaves from the stalks, discarding the stalks. Set the leaves aside.

To make the dressing, pour the milk into a small pot and bring to a boil. Whisk in the Cheddar, vinegar, and butter until all melted. Add the cornstarch, keep whisking, and bring back to a boil until the sauce is the consistency of custard. Stir in 1 tablespoon (20 ml, 1 fl oz) water and add the almonds. Keep warm.

Heat a large frying pan over high heat. Add 2 tablespoons (20 ml, 1 fl oz) of the canola oil and heat for another 2–3 minutes, until the oil is almost smoking. Add the kale and toss it around in the pan for about 30 seconds to 1 minute. You want to scorch the kale and totally wilt it.

Meanwhile, heat a small frying pan over medium heat. Add the remaining canola oil and fry the eggs, sunny-side up.

Place the kale in a large mixing bowl. Add half the dressing, including lots of the almonds and the parsley. Season with salt and freshly ground black pepper.

Spread the kale mixture onto serving plates. Dress with a little more dressing, sprinkle all over with grated Parmesan, then top with the fried eggs.

A perfect lunch dish or supper.

NOTE: For other wonderful ways to enjoy the Cheddar and Almond Dressing, see the salad dressing family tree on page 183.

CURED MACKEREL, NASTURTIUM, COCONUT & RHUBARB

This is a dish from the nighttime menu at Pope Joan. I truly love it, and its inspiration comes from a dinner my good friend Mads Refslund and I did years ago. It sounds a little strange, but hey, so are Mads and me … **Serves 4 as a plated starter**

INGREDIENTS

5 organic rhubarb stalks

2 tablespoons superfine (caster) sugar

juice of 2 lemons

1 young coconut

1 mackerel, skin on, filleted and pin-boned, then cut in half lengthways; if unavailable, try bonito or a small kingfish fillet

2 burrata balls (a soft, creamy fresh mozzarella)

3 radishes, trimmed and cut into thin matchsticks

12 nasturtium leaves, washed

8 nasturtium flowers

½ teaspoon dried shiitake mushroom salt (or you can grind 2 dried shiitake mushrooms in a spice grinder with 2 tablespoons sea salt)

METHOD

Wash and finely chop the rhubarb, then place in a small pot with the sugar and half the lemon juice. Stew gently over medium heat until all broken down, about 12–16 minutes, keeping a close eye on the rhubarb and stirring all the time. Take off the heat to cool. This is a lovely way to stew rhubarb, like me Nan used to do. It makes quite a bit, but keep it in the fridge for up to 1 week and have it for breakfast.

Take the young coconut and smash it open, reserving the juice. Then gently scrape out the flesh using a teaspoon. Give the coconut a little wash in the juice, then discard the juice.

When ready to serve, sprinkle the mackerel with the remaining lemon juice and let sit for 2–3 minutes to absorb. Slice each fillet into five pieces. If you have a kitchen blowtorch handy, use it to crisp up the skin of the mackerel; otherwise, just serve it raw.

Tear the burrata over each serving plate. Dollop the rhubarb around the plate, add the mackerel, then lay pieces of coconut and radish around. Scatter with the nasturtium leaves and flowers, then season plentifully with the mushroom salt.

Great with a riesling or a chardonnay.

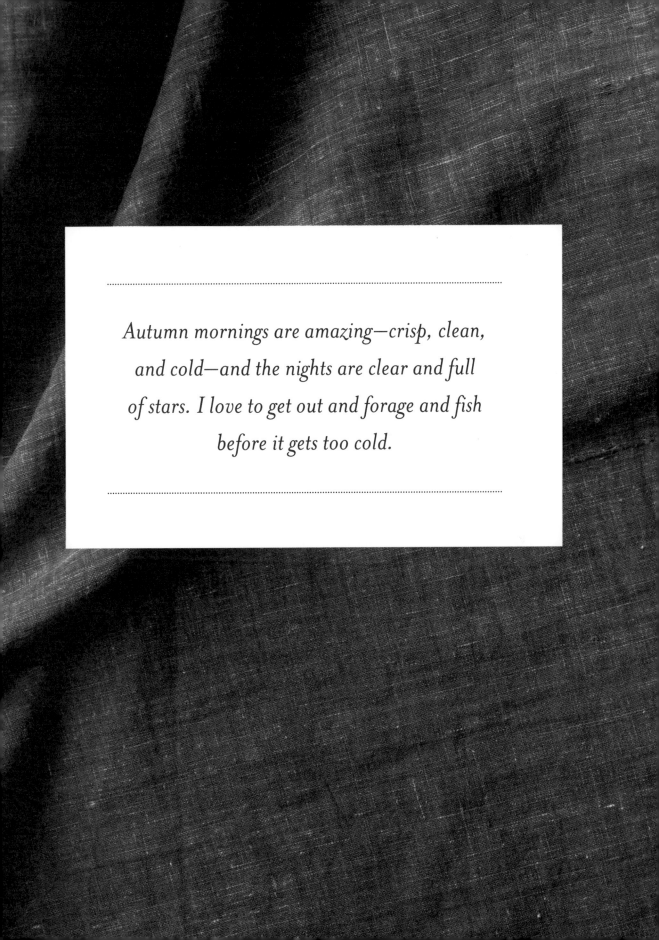

Autumn mornings are amazing—crisp, clean, and cold—and the nights are clear and full of stars. I love to get out and forage and fish before it gets too cold.

LATE AUTUMN

The cold and damp have started to set in, but there are still some cracking days of warmth and sunlight. Winter is nearing, but we are still hunting for mushrooms and using lots of amazing root vegetables, such as radishes, beets, and my love—the humble carrot—from our brilliant growers. My proud growing moment is here, admiring my brilliant fennel, planted at the right time during the summer so it didn't go to seed. I'm digging out and using my horseradishes. The flower heads of the Jerusalem artichokes have died and I'm harvesting another bumper crop out of the soil; whether in soups, salads, or garnishes for main dishes, I love the knobbly little buggers.

LEFTOVER ROAST LAMB, GRATED CARROT, TOASTED COCONUT & RAISINS

So many fond memories of my Nana Rita's roasted lamb leg—such a treat. Nowadays we don't eat much lamb, but if you have any leftovers, thinly slice the meat and lay on a plate. Grate a large carrot into a bowl; into this tear some mint, parsley, and cilantro leaves, to which I add some toasted coconut (not too much though!) and some good raisins. Mix together with a splash of good white wine vinegar and some plain yogurt, then place over your lamb. A great salad for dinner or lunch with some grilled bread.

AN OLD MAN'S SLAW

Generally, we eat salads in the summer, but think of coleslaw—everything in it is seasonal and at its best in the colder months. I love this kind of slaw—raw, crunchy, and so flavorsome. Make it up as you go along, just use this as a base ... I truly love this slaw in between two slices of buttered bread with some blue cheese. **Serves 4–6 sharing**

INGREDIENTS

1 tablespoon cumin seeds

1 tablespoon fennel seeds

1 small wedge of white cabbage, thinly sliced

1 small wedge of red cabbage, thinly sliced

1 small celeriac (celery root), peeled and cut into matchsticks

1 carrot, cut into matchsticks

5 plump radishes, trimmed and thinly sliced

1 apple, cut into matchsticks

4 tablespoons salted capers, rinsed, or chopped caperberries

2 large handfuls mixed soft leaf herbs, such as flat-leaf (Italian) parsley, dill, tarragon, and chervil, washed and chopped

good drizzle of extra-virgin olive oil

good drizzle of quality white vinegar

good sprinkling of salt

1 small piece of Parmesan, finely grated

1 small red beet, peeled and grated (or use a golden beet to avoid the color bleeding, if you wish)

METHOD

Put the cumin seeds in a small frying pan and toast over medium heat for a few minutes, tossing regularly, until they smell fragrant. Tip into a bowl.

Now toast the fennel seeds in the pan for a few minutes, tossing regularly, until fragrant. Add to the cumin seeds and lightly crush to release the flavor.

In a large mixing bowl, toss everything together except the beets. Make sure the seasoning is right, the acidity balance is right, and the salad is dressed enough. Give it a good toss. At the last minute, add the beets (this is to stop the coleslaw becoming pink). Place in a salad bowl and serve.

I have had many a good version of this coleslaw with things added and taken away, but it has always been raw—no mayo or cream near it. A simple raw slaw.

EGG, GREEN OLIVE & DUKKAH SALAD

I think everybody has a memory of eating egg salad as a child. I know I do. There is something special about cracking the egg and rolling it, ready to peel, that gives me a little childish buzz. **Serves 2–4**

INGREDIENTS

8 large free-range eggs, at room temperature

2 shallots, finely diced

12 large green olives, as brightly colored as possible, pitted

1 tablespoon salted capers, rinsed

1 garlic clove, roughly chopped

juice of 1 lemon

½ cup (100 ml, 4 fl oz) olive oil

1 teaspoon finely chopped tarragon

1 teaspoon finely chopped flat-leaf (Italian) parsley

salt to taste

freshly ground black pepper

pinch of smoked paprika

2 tablespoons Dukkah (see page 30)

METHOD

Place a pot of water on the stove and bring to a boil. Gently add the eggs and cook for 7 minutes. Remove using a slotted spoon, then wash under cold running water until cool.

Soak the shallot in hot water for 5 minutes, then drain and set aside.

Meanwhile, using a mortar and pestle, grind to a paste the olives, capers, and garlic. Gently fold in the lemon juice, olive oil, tarragon, and parsley. Season with salt and freshly ground black pepper.

Peel the eggs and chop into big bits. Place in a mixing bowl, then gently mix in the shallot and 4–5 tablespoons of the olive paste. Place on serving plates, then sprinkle with the smoked paprika and dukkah. BOOM.

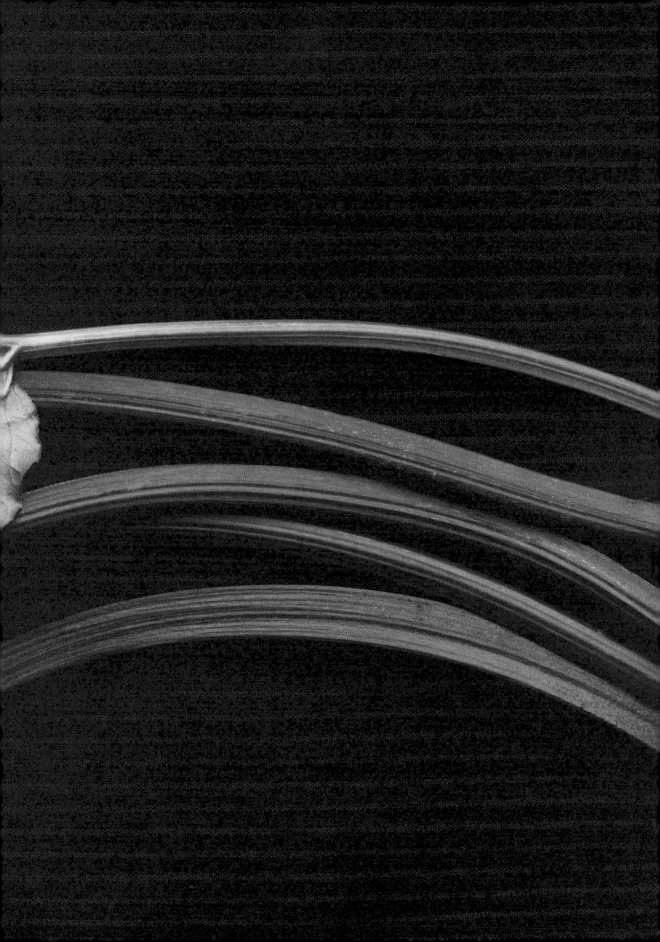

AUTUMN

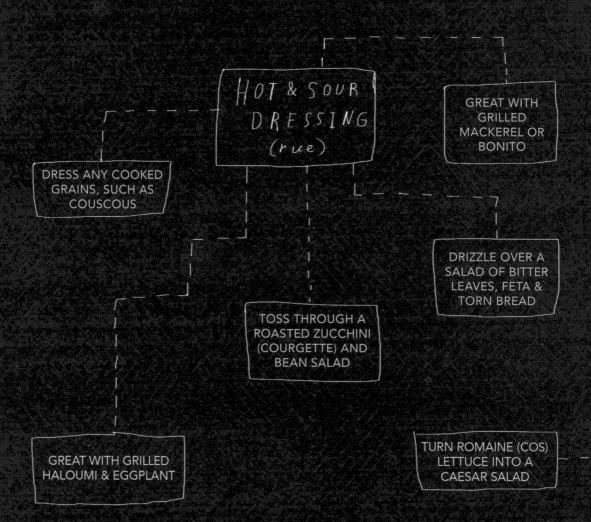

HOT & SOUR DRESSING (rue)

GREAT WITH GRILLED MACKEREL OR BONITO

DRESS ANY COOKED GRAINS, SUCH AS COUSCOUS

DRIZZLE OVER A SALAD OF BITTER LEAVES, FETA & TORN BREAD

TOSS THROUGH A ROASTED ZUCCHINI (COURGETTE) AND BEAN SALAD

GREAT WITH GRILLED HALOUMI & EGGPLANT

TURN ROMAINE (COS) LETTUCE INTO A CAESAR SALAD

MIX WITH CUT APPLE & PEAR, FIGS & CELERY

ROLL HOT CHICKEN DRUMSTICKS IN THE DRESSING AND SERVE WITH A SIMPLE SALAD

AUTUMN

STIR THROUGH GNOCCHI WITH FRIED BACON

USE IT AS A FONDUE IN WHICH TO DIP BREAD

CHEDDAR & ALMOND DRESSING (Kale)

FOLD THROUGH FENNEL AND LIGHTLY BAKE

CHILL THE DRESSING STUFF INTO MUSHROOMS, ADD BREADCRUMBS, AND BAKE

USE IN A CORNED BEEF, CAULIFLOWER & POTATO BUBBLE 'N' SQUEAK

DRIZZLE OVER POACHED FISH OR ROASTED PORK

ANCHOVY DRESSING (Potato Salad)

LOVELY WITH DICED LEFTOVER CHICKEN, PUT IN A SANDWICH WITH SOME CURRANTS

TORN FRESH FIGS & GRAPES WITH ALMONDS & STRAWBERRY BALSAMIC

Whether used in dishes savory or sweet, figs just rock. I warm the fruit in the oven to give the figs a sun-warmed feel. I like it … a lot! **Serves 2**

INGREDIENTS

6 ripe figs

1 small bunch green grapes (I like to use muscatel seedless)

1 tablespoon chopped almonds

1 tablespoon superfine (caster) sugar

2 tablespoons strawberry balsamic vinegar or plain balsamic vinegar

7 oz (200 g) mascarpone

METHOD

Preheat the oven to 350°F (180°C, Gas 4).

Tear each fig into three bits and place in a small baking dish. Tear the grapes in half, or cut them using a small knife, then add to the figs. Add the almonds and sugar and toss lightly. Place in the oven for 3–4 minutes, just to lightly warm the fruit.

Divide the fruit mixture among serving plates or bowls. Drizzle with the balsamic vinegar. Add a good scoop of mascarpone and serve.

BASIL
CORDIAL

INGREDIENTS

4 cups (750g, 1lb 11oz) sugar

1 tablespoon (15g, ½ oz)
citric acid (see glossary)

2 large bunches
basil leaves & stalks
(150g, 5 oz)

BASIL CORDIAL

This recipe is inspired by a lovely Swiss lady, Anita, from Mimi's Kitchen in Murchison, county Victoria, who sells her cordials and dressings in our shop, Hams & Bacon. Why basil in autumn? What better way to use up all that surplus basil growing in the garden that will all be gone soon … **Makes 5½ cups (1¼ liters, 42½ fl oz)**

METHOD

Pour 4 cups (1 liter, 34 fl oz) water into a large pot. Add the sugar and citric acid and bring to a boil, stirring to make sure all the sugar has dissolved.

Smash the basil stalks with the back of a knife to release the flavor. Place them in a heatproof bowl with the basil leaves, then pour the hot liquid over them.

Cover the bowl and leave to infuse at room temperature until cool. Pass the mixture through a fine sieve back into a pot. Bring back to a boil, then pour into sterilized jars and seal.

Keep in a cool dark place for up to 4 months. Once opened, store in the fridge and use within 3 weeks.

RHUBARB, APPLE & GINGER CORDIAL

After writing book number one, it was pointed out to me by the lovely Jo, who supplies our amazing organic rhubarb from Bridge Farm, that rhubarb is actually a vegetable. Fascinating. I should have done a whole chapter on it. I love rhubarb, and this cordial reminds me a little of the boiled sweets I used to buy at the corner shop when I was a nipper. **Makes 6⅓ cups (1½ liters, 51 fl oz)**

METHOD

In a large pot, combine the rhubarb, ginger, lemon juice, and ¾ cup plus 2 tablespoons (200 ml, 7 fl oz) water. Leave to cook over low heat for about 10–12 minutes, until the rhubarb has started to break down. Cool, then blitz in a blender.

Return the mixture to a clean pot. Add the remaining ingredients, bring to a boil, then reduce the heat and simmer for 10 minutes.

Scoop away any impurities from the top using a spoon, then pour into sterilized jars and seal.

Keep in a cool dark place for up to 6 months. Once opened, store in the fridge and use within 6 weeks.

WINTER

WINTER

AH, WINTER. THE COLDEST SEASON, WHEN PEOPLE SUDDENLY THINK IT'S OKAY TO WEAR SOCKS TO BED (UGH!).

I tend to feel a bit older in winter—creaking bones and creaking floorboards. It reminds me of living in Edinburgh when I was an apprentice chef and having no heating. Getting into bed and snuggling down and never wanting to get up. And when I did get up, wrapping myself in seven layers and getting lost in scarves, hats, and gloves.

Still, nothing beats opening up your curtains in the morning and seeing snow. There is an amazing light in winter, one that is clear and crisp. The colors of snow, so white that it is almost blue. The leaves have fallen from the deciduous trees, and everything looks dormant and lifeless. When you walk outside on a clear winter day, the air is so fresh and bracing that you can feel it burning all the way from your nostrils into your lungs. And it is filled with the smell of smoke from other people's open fires, which is always so inviting. It's the most hypnotic thing to sit in front of an open fire and watch the flames leaping over each other.

In the northern hemisphere, the animals are hibernating—like the little hedgehogs, my favorite! Creatures hibernate here in Australia too, though we don't associate hibernation with the southern hemisphere as much. All the eels and yabbies head into their burrows in the waterways, staying inside until it starts to warm up again in spring. And the bees and the butterflies have disappeared. Where do they go?

It is the end of the cycle—and also the beginning of the cycle—of life and of rebirth. For this reason the winter solstice, the shortest day of the year, is celebrated in many cultures across the world. This day is seen as a turning point from which the sun gets brighter and stronger as the year progresses. It was considered a particularly sacred time in the yearly cycle of life—a time of reflection and ritual, of giving thanks and goodwill within the community. It has its roots in pagan times, when so much depended on the gifts of the seasons, and incredible importance was placed on seasonal celebration.

Even now, though we try to make the most of the reduced sunlight, everything seems to slow down in winter. We cook with the secondary cuts of meat, ones that need to be braised for long hours at a low heat. We spoil ourselves with warming whiskeys and full-bodied red wines, and eating becomes an indulgence. We eat more. Robust stews and roasts are the order of the day, along with big, hearty warming bowls of soup with chunky bread. We brew ourselves concoctions of ginger, honey, and lemon to protect our bodies from winter bugs.

And what is coming through in the garden protects us too. Citrus is in full swing in winter—loading us up with vitamin C that our body craves to ward off colds. Lemons, limes, and gorgeous winter oranges are all in fruit and bring some vibrant color into the season. And they also bring juice, ready for preserving in the form of a cordial. We tend to associate fresh lemonade with cooling us down at the height of summer, but lemons aren't actually in season in summer! It is the preserved juice from the winter crop that allows us to enjoy a refreshing lemonade on a sweltering day.

There is definitely not much happening in the winter garden; the plants are conserving their energy for the time to come. Everything slows down, and it is the slow-growing veggies—the Brassica family—that really love winter. Cabbage has been in the ground for four months, but now it sits proudly, waiting to be harvested. There is a reason why cabbage is so central to the cuisine of most of Europe—it's all about making the most of what you can get to grow. Bring on the sauerkraut, I say!

The broccoli will have been slowly growing for three months or so, and by now you should have some gorgeous heads sitting atop the woody stalks. If you want to try something different, plant some delightful Romanesco broccoli; you can pick up some seeds at any continental supermarket. They have the most crazy, delightful pointy crowns on their head.

Your cauliflower should have bloomed a big tight head, all nestled in and protected by its outer leaves and stalks. And then there's my old mate, the warty, funny looking Brussels sprout. It is a truly ugly plant, but it's so lovely to eat.

Kale is a delight of the winter garden, too, and close cousin to the cabbage. It makes headlines these days for being one of the "new" superfoods, but it has been widely enjoyed since Roman times. The cultivation of kale was encouraged by the British government during World War II as part of its "Dig for Victory" campaign, as it contained so many of the nutrients that were missing from an austere rationing diet. That, and it is super easy to grow.

All those old-fashioned vegetables, like turnips and rutabaga, make you think of your Grandma making soul-warming winter soups in the kitchen. These vitamin-dense veggies are full of the nutrients our bodies need to get us through to spring.

But there is really not much happening in the garden. It's not like the height of summer, when you really need to be in there every day, watering and tending. You can afford to be a bit more reserved in winter. The ground is hard with the cold, but now is the time to put in a bit of preparation work for the seasons ahead. Compost and manicure the garden and give it a good blanket to really protect it from the frost. It's time to think about getting your seeds into trays now, to get planted once spring rolls around.

In the kitchen, winter is the time to start pulling out all the preserves and pickles that were made and put away with all of summer's excess produce. There is a limit to the amount of produce that will grow in the winter, so it is always good to be able to supplement what you have with what you have preserved. It's time to cut into last year's salamis and to pull out the jarred stonefruits for your warming winter pies and crumbles. You'll be glad you went to the effort, believe me!

CARROTS, THEIR TOPS, HONEY & SMOKED YOGURT

As I said in my first book, carrots are my favorite vegetable. I have always done a version of carrots as a salad, and this is the new dish we have been doing now for some time. It was inspired by the second best-looking chef ever, after me—the sexy Darren Robertson, my good mate from Three Blue Ducks restaurant in Sydney. You're a legend, bud. **Serves 2–4 sharing**

INGREDIENTS

¾ cup (160 g, 5½ oz) Smoked Yogurt (see page 35), or use plain yogurt but don't add the milk below

2 tablespoons (20 ml, 1 fl oz) milk

24 baby heirloom carrots, washed well, leafy green tops reserved for the pesto (see below)

olive oil, for drizzling

CARROT TOP PESTO

1 small handful flat-leaf (Italian) parsley, leaves only, washed

4 garlic cloves, peeled

2 tablespoons Dukkah (see page 30), plus extra for sprinkling

1 tablespoon almonds

1 tablespoon blonde sultanas (golden raisins)

1 tablespoon grated Parmesan

good pinch of salt

3 tablespoons (40 ml, 1½ fl oz) chardonnay vinegar (see glossary)

1 tablespoon honey

⅔ cup (150 ml, 5 fl oz) olive oil

2 teaspoons orange flower water (see glossary)

METHOD

Preheat the oven to 375°F (190°C, Gas 5). In a bowl, mix together the smoked yogurt and milk. Set aside.

Heat a grill pan or grill to high. Place the green carrot tops in a bowl and drizzle with some olive oil. Char the carrot greens on the grill for a few minutes until all nicely browned, then remove and set aside for the pesto.

Now char the whole baby carrots for about 5 minutes, until nicely charred all over. Place on a baking tray and bake for 8–12 minutes, or until just tender but still a bit crunchy.

To make the carrot top pesto, place the charred carrot tops in a blender with the parsley, garlic, and a tablespoon or two of water. Blitz. Now add the dukkah, almonds, sultanas, Parmesan, and salt and blitz again to form a paste. Add the vinegar, honey, olive oil, and orange flower water and blitz again until smooth.

Once the carrots are cooked, cut them into random shapes, or just leave them whole. Place in a mixing bowl and dress with a good amount of the pesto.

Spread the smoked yogurt around a serving plate, then top with the carrots and sprinkle with some extra dukkah. Serve with some more pesto on the side.

The plants are conserving their energy for the time to come. The ground is hard with the cold, but now is the time to put in a bit of preparation work for the seasons ahead.

CURED KINGFISH WITH RYE & BEETS

Curing your own fish is really beautiful and, honestly, very easy. Even if you don't make this salad recipe, have a go at curing the fish and enjoying it as a snack. The curing recipe works just as well for snapper and salmon, too. **Serves 4 as a plated starter**

INGREDIENTS

2 extra large red beets, peeled and cut into ½-inch (1 cm) cubes

1 ripe avocado

1 tablespoon crème fraîche or Greek-style yogurt

salt to taste

1 small royal gala apple, washed but not peeled, cut into matchsticks

1 small handful watercress sprigs, washed

1 tablespoon salted capers, rinsed

dill sprigs, to garnish

juice of 1 lemon

2 tablespoons (20 ml, 1 fl oz) olive oil

1 thick slice rye bread, the darker the better, toasted and crumbled

CURED KINGFISH

10½ oz (300 g) kingfish fillet, skin and bloodline removed, pin-boned (ask your fishmonger to do this)

½ cup plus 2 tablespoons (150 g, 5½ oz) superfine (caster) sugar

½ cup plus 2 tablespoons (150 g, 5½ oz) salt

zest of 1 lemon

2 tablespoons chopped dill

METHOD

To cure the fish, place the fillet on a tray or in a container large enough to hold it (preferably one with a lid). Mix together the sugar, salt, lemon zest, and dill, then cover all sides of the fish with this mixture. Cover and place in the fridge for 4 hours. After this time, take the fish out of the salt mixture and wash well under cold water to remove all the mixture. Pat dry and thinly slice. Place on a tray and refrigerate until serving time.

Place the beets in a saucepan, cover with cold water, and bring to a boil. Reduce the heat and simmer for 5–8 minutes, or until cooked. Drain and cool.

Just before serving, remove the peel and pit from the avocado. Blitz the avocado flesh and crème fraîche together using a handheld immersion blender into a smooth paste. Season to taste with salt.

To serve, dollop the avocado mixture onto serving plates. Layer the kingfish slices randomly all over, then place the beets around. Arrange the apple and watercress over, then add the capers and dill sprigs. Drizzle with the lemon juice and olive oil, sprinkle with the rye crumbs and serve.

EARLY WINTER

The vibrant colors of the many varieties of citrus give light to a time when the cold and gloom sets in. Mandarins, clementines, navel oranges, ruby grapefruit, lemons, lemonade fruit, limes, and kaffir limes, just to name a few. My mum always gave us half a grapefruit to eat in winter for breakfast (which Mum, if you read this, can I tell you was a bad idea after you made us brush our teeth—toothpaste and citrus just don't go together). It will be another month until my favorite of all the citrus, the blood orange, comes into season, but I can wait when there is so much flavor of the other citrus varieties around.

The leaves are off most of the trees, and it is the time to rake them up and place them into your compost. Many of my old Italian and Greek neighbors walk the streets at this time collecting the piles of yellow, orange, and many hues of brown from the roadside.

HOT SMOKED SALMON, GRATED BEETS, CAPERS & SOUR CREAM

I love using smoked salmon, whether it be cold or hot smoked. I use salmon from New Zealand, from Regal and Ora King, an amazing fishery that uses the Chinook breed and brilliant farming techniques, which give an incredible flavor, with such a rich fat content it makes them superb for smoking. So, flake a big piece of hot smoked salmon into a bowl. Grate 1 large peeled beet into another bowl, then drizzle with the juice of a lemon, a good shaving of fresh horseradish, some washed salted capers, chopped dill and parsley, sea salt, freshly ground black pepper, and a sprinkle of olive oil.
Mix, then carefully fold the salmon through. Place on a plate, dollop sour cream over, and boom! Great as a wintry nighttime dish, or in between two slices of a grainy sourdough bread.

CRUMBED CODDLED EGGS WITH BLACK PUDDING SALAD

A salad for breakfast? "He is crazy!" I hear you cry. Yep. This was one of the first dishes we served at Pope Joan back in 2010. It's a ripper—basically a take on a Caesar salad.

If you don't like black pudding, harden up. It's amazing and such a delicate, flavorsome food.

Serves 4

INGREDIENTS

1 tablespoon (15 ml, ½ fl oz) white vinegar

4 extra-large free-range eggs

2 cups (200 g, 7 oz) dry breadcrumbs

¾ cup (180 ml, 6 fl oz) buttermilk

1 tablespoon dijon mustard

4 cups (1 liter, 34 fl oz) vegetable oil

4 slices sourdough bread, toasted

ANCHOVY DRESSING

1 small can (48 g, 1¾ oz) anchovy fillets

¼ cup (50 ml, 2 fl oz) chardonnay vinegar (see glossary)

½ cup (100 ml, 4 fl oz) sunflower oil

BLACK PUDDING SALAD

3 tablespoons (40 ml, 1½ fl oz) sunflower oil

4½ oz (125 g) bacon or pancetta, cut into batons

2 7 oz (200 g) black puddings, each cut into 8 pieces

1 small handful watercress sprigs, washed

1 small handful baby arugula (rocket) leaves, washed

1 handful flat-leaf (Italian) parsley, picked and washed

METHOD

First we are going to poach the eggs, then chill them down straight away, so you will need a bowl of cold water containing as much ice as you have (I know it's probably not much, if your freezer ice trays are like mine).

Add the vinegar to a pot of water and bring to a boil. Reduce the heat to a simmer. Using a spoon, turn the water counterclockwise, then gently crack the eggs into the simmering water. Poach for 3–3½ minutes, or until the whites are cooked, but the yolks are still runny. Remove with a slotted spoon, straight into the iced water. Once cool, remove from the water and pat dry with a tea towel (dish towel).

We are now going to crumb the eggs! Place the breadcrumbs in a bowl. In another bowl, whisk together the buttermilk and mustard. Place the eggs first into the buttermilk mixture, then into the breadcrumbs. Repeat with each egg, then crumb again following the same technique. Set aside.

To make the dressing, blitz together the anchovies, vinegar, and sunflower oil, using a handheld immersion blender. Set aside.

Now let's get started on the black pudding salad. Heat a large frying pan over medium heat, add half the sunflower oil, and cook the bacon until crispy. Remove from the pan and set aside to cool.

Heat the remaining oil in the pan and fry the black pudding slices until crispy on both sides and hot in the middle. Set aside.

Carefully, in a deep saucepan, warm the vegetable oil to 350°F (180°C), using a cooking thermometer as a guide. Deep-fry the eggs for 2–3 minutes, until the coating is crispy.

To serve, place the sourdough toasts on serving plates, then arrange the fried black pudding around. Place the watercress, arugula, parsley, and crispy bacon in a mixing bowl and coat with the dressing. Arrange the salad over the plates, then top each one with a crumbed coddled egg. Serve hot.

MY SAAG ALOO, WITH OR WITHOUT FRIED EGG

Growing up in Yorkshire, England, was a delight. One of the many reasons was that we were surrounded by so many good Indian restaurants. I don't know why, but saag aloo (spinach and potatoes) was a dish I always ordered—that and a few pints of beer. This is my version, which we eat quite often at home.
Serves 2–4 sharing

INGREDIENTS

2 lb 3 oz (1 kg) good boiling potatoes (I like to use Dutch creams for this dish), peeled and cut into ¾-inch (2 cm) cubes

⅓ cup (80 ml, 2½ fl oz) olive oil

5½ tablespoons (75 g, 2¾ oz) butter

1 large white onion, sliced

5 garlic cloves, sliced

1 teaspoon mixed mustard seeds

1 teaspoon cumin seeds

½ teaspoon ground turmeric

½ teaspoon ground ginger

½ teaspoon cracked black pepper

good pinch of salt

1 large handful baby spinach leaves, washed

METHOD

Put the potatoes in a pot filled with water and bring to a boil. Reduce the heat and simmer for 4–6 minutes, or until the potatoes are just cooked, or even a little undercooked. Drain and set aside.

Add the olive oil and butter to a saucepan and place on high heat. Once the butter has melted and started to turn from clear to brown, add the onion and garlic and turn the heat down to low. Slowly cook the onion, without letting it color, for 6–7 minutes. Now add all the spices and cook really slowly for a good 3 minutes, stirring occasionally.

Add the cooked potatoes to the pot and cook for a further 2–3 minutes. Take off the heat straight away, add the salt, and fold in the spinach. Now put a lid on and let sit for a good 5–10 minutes, until the spinach has wilted. Stir gently again and you're ready to serve.

I like the saag aloo with a fried egg on top—again a great breakfast salad or brunch snack—but add some grilled Indian bread and some minted yogurt and it's a great salad for dinner.

Any leftovers are great as a cold salad, too, next day at work.

MY WALDORF-STYLE SALAD OF BRUSSELS SPROUTS & GUANCIALE

Okay, so the only thing that makes this salad remotely waldorf-like is the celery, apple and walnuts… but that's the great thing about cooking. A few changes here and there, based around a simple foundation, and you have another lovely dish. **Serves 2–4**

INGREDIENTS

8 thin slices jowl bacon (guanciale) (see glossary) or pancetta, from your butcher

2 teaspoons confectioners' (icing) sugar

½ cup (50 g, 1¾ oz) walnuts

7 oz (200 g) Brussels sprouts

1 small apple, cut into matchsticks

2 large celery stalks, peeled and sliced on an angle

ENGLISH MUSTARD DRESSING

1½ teaspoons hot English mustard

¼ cup (50 ml, 2 fl oz) chardonnay vinegar (see glossary)

⅔ cup (150 ml, 5 fl oz) light (pouring, single) cream

pinch of salt

pinch of sugar

METHOD

Preheat the oven to 350°F (180°C, Gas 4). Place a sheet of baking parchment on a baking tray and lay the bacon slices on top. Carefully dust the confectioners' sugar all over the bacon, then bake for 7–9 minutes, or until crispy. Take out of the oven and let cool.

Meanwhile, spread the walnuts on a baking tray and bake for 3–4 minutes, or until lightly toasted and fragrant. Remove from the oven, roughly chop the nuts, then set aside.

For the Brussels sprouts, peel off and reserve the outer layers of leaves (discarding any crappy looking leaves), until you get to the inner part. Using a mandoline, finely shave the middle part of the Brussels sprouts, then place in a mixing bowl.

Now bring a pot of water to a boil. Add the reserved outer leaves, bring back to a boil, then take off the heat. Strain the leaves and rinse under cold running water until cool. Shake the water off the blanched leaves, then add to the bowl of shaved leaves.

Whisk all the dressing ingredients together in a bowl, then dress the Brussels sprouts and gently mix together. Add three-quarters of the apple, celery, and toasted walnuts.

Place in a serving bowl. Garnish with the remaining apple, celery, and walnuts, then crumble the bacon over. Delish.

BAKED BROCCOLI WITH GOAT'S CURD, HORSERADISH & BACON VINAIGRETTE

Broccoli is such a diverse and lovely tasting vegetable. I love working with it—raw, cooked, as a soup—it's all mighty fine. This is a recipe from a while ago, when we did special Wednesday night winter dinners, and is served as a warm salad to share. **Serves 4 sharing**

INGREDIENTS

½ cup (100 ml, 4 fl oz) olive oil

2 small heads of broccoli, cut in half lengthways

5½ oz (150 g) goat's curd or very fresh goat cheese

1 quantity of Bacon Vinaigrette (see page 54)

3 Pickled Shallots (see page 31)

1 tablespoon chopped almonds

TOASTED PARMESAN CRUMBS

1 cup (80 g, 2¾ oz) fresh breadcrumbs

2½ tablespoons (40 ml, 1¼ oz) melted butter

pinch of cayenne pepper

1 garlic clove, peeled and finely grated

1 teaspoon grated fresh horseradish, or 1 teaspoon horseradish paste

1 tablespoon grated Parmesan

METHOD

Preheat the oven to 375°F (190°C, Gas 5).

Place a frying pan over high heat. Add the olive oil. Working in batches, fry the broccoli, cut side down, for a few minutes, until golden brown.

Place all the broccoli in a deep-sided baking dish, flat side facing up. To the dish add 2 cups (500 ml, 17 fl oz) water. Transfer to the oven and bake for 10–15 minutes, or until the broccoli is fully cooked.

Meanwhile, toast the Parmesan crumbs. To do this, mix all the ingredients in a bowl until well combined. Spread the crumbs on a baking tray and bake for 6–8 minutes, or until golden, shaking the tray every few minutes so they color evenly.

To serve, arrange the broccoli on a serving platter. Spoon the goat's curd around. Dress with the bacon vinaigrette, add some pickled shallot, then sprinkle the toasted crumbs and almonds all over.

MIDWINTER

All is not bad in the garden, well for me anyway, here in Melbourne. I'm actually chuffed at how well my cabbages, broccoli, cauliflower, and kale are doing. The leeks and onions are looking splendid as well, but it's time I pruned a few things, in case there's an early bud burst the month before spring. And I should, if the weather is nice on the weekend, really compost the strawberries and mulch everywhere. It's cold and dark in the morning when I wake, and dark on my way home, but the smell of burning wood fires wafting through the air is a delight.

Blood oranges are here and it's time to crack open some of my summer in a jar—my homemade sugo—and make a pasta, maybe with a refreshing arugula and radicchio leaf salad that I harvest straight from the garden. Salad leaves taste so good in winter.

LEFTOVER PORK ROAST, TAPENADE, BROCCOLI, GRAINS & HALOUMI

Another leftover dish. Leftover meats really do lend themselves to salads, and for this one, I simply boil some grains—generally a good cup of lentils, cracked wheat, or pearl barley. Once cooked, I fold through some raw, finely grated broccoli, and the pork leftovers that I've pulled or diced into chunks. Then I make a quick tapenade by blitzing together 1 cup of pitted black olives, enough olive oil to cover them, 1 chopped garlic clove, 3 anchovies, and the juice of half a lemon. Dress the salad with the tapenade, panfry some thick slices of haloumi until golden on each side, then lay on a plate and spoon the salad over.

GRILLED BABY LEEKS, CHICKEN LIVERS & ROMESCO SAUCE

A dish inspired by my good friend Stevie Parle from the United Kingdom. Stevie cooks from the heart and cooks food that has inspired him from his global travels. This dish is a mix of two dishes he did at Pope Joan in 2012. **Serves 2–4 as a starter**

INGREDIENTS

10½ oz (300 g) chicken livers, trimmed by your butcher

1 tablespoon pomegranate molasses

1 teaspoon ras el hanout (see glossary)

2 tablespoons (20 ml, 1 fl oz) olive oil, plus extra for drizzling

2 large leeks, white part only, roots trimmed

1 quantity of Romesco Sauce (see page 32)

1 small handful flat-leaf (Italian) parsley, washed and torn

good pinch of ground sumac (see glossary)

METHOD

Preheat the oven to 375ºF (190ºC, Gas 5).

Heat a grill pan to high. In a bowl, mix together the chicken livers, pomegranate molasses, ras el hanout, and olive oil. Let sit while finishing the leeks.

Cut the leeks in half lengthways, rinse out any grit, and pat dry with paper towels. Drizzle the leeks with a little extra olive oil, then place on the hot grill pan, cut side down, and char until lightly browned all over—about 3–4 minutes total. Now place on a baking tray and bake for 7–10 minutes, or until you can insert a sharp knife through easily. Remove from the oven and set aside.

Place the chicken livers on the hot grill pan, turn the heat down to medium and cook on one side for 2–3 minutes, or until beautifully browned. Turn them over, lower the heat, and cook the livers through. This should take another 3–4 minutes. Take off the heat and let rest for 3–5 minutes.

Dollop some of the romesco sauce onto a plate, then arrange the leeks alongside. Add the chicken livers—you can cut them up a little if you need to—then finish with the parsley and a sprinkling of sumac.

CARROTS COOKED IN THEIR OWN JUICE WITH LABNEH & PICKLED CHILI

This dish is all about the taste of the carrots. Try before you buy! Take a good bite out of one at the shop, or buy from a producer who grows the tasty stuff. These carrots are wonderful with baked or steamed fish. **Serves 4**

INGREDIENTS

6 large carrots, about 1¾ lb (800 g)

3 oranges, peeled

¾-inch (2 cm) knob of fresh ginger, peeled and chopped (about 20 g, 1 oz)

½ cup (100 ml, 4 fl oz) sweet wine, or verjuice (see glossary) if not available

¼ cup (50 ml, 2 fl oz) chardonnay vinegar (see glossary)

salt to taste

1 tablespoon unsalted butter, diced

freshly ground black pepper

½ cup (100 g, 4 oz) labneh (see glossary), or Smoked Yogurt (see page 35)

3 hot pickled green chilies (from a jar), finely chopped; use more or less to suit your taste

½ teaspoon coriander seeds, toasted and gently crushed

METHOD

Look at the carrots, be at one with the carrots ... then cut the tops off and peel them.

Cut three carrots into small finger-width rounds, putting the tail bits with the other three carrots. Now, using a juicer, juice the remaining carrots, the oranges, and ginger.

Place the sliced carrots into a pan that they will all fit in. Mix the wine and vinegar with the carrot juice mixture, season with salt, then pour over the carrots. Bring to the boil, then reduce the heat. Now simmer gently, scooping off any impurities with a spoon, and every now and then spooning some of the juices over the carrots as the liquid starts to reduce. It should take a good 20–30 minutes until the carrots are cooked and tender.

Carefully spoon out the carrots and arrange on a plate, ready to serve.

Reduce the remaining liquid for a few more minutes, if necessary, to give you a glaze the consistency of cream. Transfer to a small, clean saucepan and warm over low heat, then whisk in the butter to thicken. Taste, season with salt and freshly ground black pepper, and add a little more vinegar if you like it a bit sharper. This is your carrot dressing.

Spoon the warm dressing over the carrots and plate. Spoon some labneh onto the carrots. Scatter with the chili, sprinkle with the toasted coriander seeds, and serve.

SPICED ROASTED PUMPKIN & FALAFEL SALAD

Another lovely take on a daytime special at Pope Joan. I have to admit I wasn't the biggest fan of falafel until I tasted this dish. **Serves 2 as a starter, or 2–4 sharing**

INGREDIENTS

2 cups (300 g, 10½ oz) falafel mix (from health food shops and Middle Eastern grocers)

1 small onion, finely diced

1 small handful curly parsley, washed and roughly chopped

1 small handful mint, washed and chopped

good pinch of salt

2 lb 3 oz (1 kg) sugar or other sweet pumpkin (winter squash), peeled, seeded, and cut into 1-inch (2.5 cm) cubes

2 teaspoons baharat spice blend (see glossary) or ras el hanout (see glossary)

1 teaspoon salt

1¼ cups (340 ml, 11 fl oz) olive oil, plus extra for drizzling

1 small handful arugula (rocket) leaves

½ ball shanklish (see glossary)

GREEN OLIVE DRESSING

4 oz (100 g) green kalamata olives, pitted and roughly chopped

1 garlic clove, peeled

1 large handful mixed mint, parsley, and dill, washed and chopped

zest and juice of 1 lemon

½ cup (100 ml, 4 fl oz) olive oil

METHOD

Place the falafel mix, onion, and herbs in a food processor. Add a good pinch of salt and ¾ cup (180 ml, 6 fl oz) water. Blend for 3 minutes, until everything is combined. Scoop into a bowl, let rest in the fridge for 15 minutes, then roll into balls the size of walnuts. Set aside.

Meanwhile, preheat the oven to 375ºF (190ºC, Gas 5).

In a mixing bowl, toss together the pumpkin, baharat, and salt. Drizzle with a little olive oil and scatter over a baking tray. Bake for 12–16 minutes, or until tender, then take out of the oven and let cool a little.

To make the dressing, use a mortar and pestle to smash the olives, garlic, herbs, lemon zest, and lemon juice to a paste. Fold in the olive oil with a spoon.

In a large deep frying pan, heat the olive oil over medium heat. Make sure the oil is hot, then fry the falafels in batches for 3–4 minutes, or until crispy on the outside and fully cooked through.

Dress your serving plate with the green olive dressing. Arrange the falafels on the plate. Mix the roasted pumpkin and arugula together, then scatter all over the plate, adding a little more dressing if needed. Tear the shanklish over and serve.

NOTE: For other fabulous uses for the Green Olive Dressing, see the salad dressing family tree on page 233.

WARM SALAD OF FREGOLA, CHORIZO & MUSSELS

Fregola is also known as Sardinian couscous and is very similar to Israeli couscous. For another dish, cook your fregola and toss through some grated pecorino, mascarpone, chopped parsley, some salt, and freshly ground black pepper, then top with a poached egg and lots of shaved truffle. Amazing.

Serves 2 or 4 sharing

INGREDIENTS

1 cup (200 g, 7 oz) fregola

¼ cup (50 ml, 2 fl oz) olive oil, plus extra for drizzling

4 oz (100 g) chorizo, finely diced

1 small carrot, finely diced

1 celery stalk, peeled and finely diced

16 large mussels, scrubbed well, hairy beards removed

2 tablespoons harissa paste

1 tablespoon chopped flat-leaf (Italian) parsley

METHOD

Bring a pot of water to a boil. Add the fregola and cook for 7–8 minutes, or until al dente. Drain and set aside in a mixing bowl.

Place a large pot over a medium heat. Add the olive oil and gently fry the chorizo, carrot, and celery for 5–6 minutes. Turn the heat up high and cook for a further 1 minute, stirring all the time.

Add the mussels, then cover the pot, and cook for 3–5 minutes, until all the mussels open. Spoon the mussels from the shells, discarding any unopened ones, and set aside.

Stir in the harissa and cook, without the lid on, for 1–2 minutes, or until the mixture has reduced to a sauce consistency. Take off the heat, pour over the fregola, and stir through.

Add the mussels and most of the parsley. Pour onto a serving plate, sprinkle with the remaining parsley, drizzle with a little more olive oil, and serve.

LATE WINTER

I'm over it now—the cold, the wet, the dark.
When will you arrive, warmer weather?
I'm sick of standing in the shower until the
pipes warm up and the cold water turns to hot.
I'm sick of clearing the front window of my car of
frost. I'm sick of the Brassica family—I don't want
to see another bloody cabbage or cauliflower
on the plate again … but hey, that's eating and
being seasonal.

That said, the first signs of change are in the
garden. The daffodils are shooting, buds are
starting to burst on some of my trees, and even
certain birds have come back to the garden. The
vine I thought I had overpruned is starting to show
shoots, and damn, I need to weed the garden.
And we really need to eat some more leafy
greens … the arugula, speckled radicchio, and
romaine lettuce are going crazy.

RECIPE:

AN AMAZING
CAESAR SALAD

My friend and former boss Lisa Van Haandel has given me her family recipe, and it's a beauty. The dressing alone should go on just about anything, but I would just dress romaine leaves with this dressing, lay them on a plate, then add fried bacon bits, chopped parsley, freshly made croutons the size of your smallest fingernail, and add a few poached eggs crowned with slices of parmesan. Brilliant in any season, but since my romaine lettuce is out of control, it's the perfect winter salad for me.

For the Caesar dressing, soak 2 chopped garlic cloves in ¼ cup (50 ml, 2 fl oz) white wine vinegar for 10 minutes. Place the whole lot in a blender with 2 egg yolks, a sprinkling of sea salt, 2 teaspoons dijon mustard, 1 tablespoon Worcestershire sauce, 2 anchovies, and a little of the oil they were swimming in. Blitz together, then add ¾ cup (180 ml, 6 fl oz) of vegetable oil and 1 tablespoon grated Parmesan. Adjust the seasoning and away you go.

PEARL BARLEY TABBOULEH & LEMON BARLEY WATER

The base concept of this tabbouleh comes from my mate David Moyle, when we were joint head chefs for a little while at Circa in Melbourne. The lemon barley water comes from the Mrs., and is a great refreshing drink any time of the year. You can change the grains around if you wish, but you'll miss out on making the lovely drink. **Serves 4; makes 8 cups (2 liters, 68 fl oz) lemon barley water**

INGREDIENTS

1 head Belgian endive (witlof, chicory), thinly sliced

2 large handfuls curly parsley, washed and chopped

2 tablespoons Dukkah (see page 30)

½ cup (60 g, 2 oz) shredded cauliflower (shredded using a grater or a mandoline)

2 shallots, finely diced

1 cup (220 g, 8 oz) pearl barley

5 lemons

3 tablespoons (40 ml, 1½ fl oz) olive oil

salt to taste

freshly ground black pepper

METHOD

In a bowl, place the endive, parsley, dukkah, cauliflower, and shallot. Set aside.

Take a really big pot and pour in 12 cups (3 liters) water. Add the barley and bring to a boil, then reduce the heat and simmer for 22–26 minutes, or until cooked. Take off the heat.

Strain the barley liquid into a bowl and set aside. Spread the grains on a tray to cool, then mix the cooled grains with the cauliflower mixture.

Peel the skin from the lemons, avoiding the bitter white pith, then add the lemon peel to the barley cooking liquid. Juice three of the lemons and add the juice to the barley liquid; juice the remaining two lemons and add the juice to the cauliflower mixture. Drizzle with the olive oil, then gently mix together. Season with salt and freshly ground black pepper ... and there's your tabbouleh!

Let the barley liquid cool, then strain into a jug. Keep in the fridge and consume within 5 days. Enjoy your lemon barley water with some ice.

SHREDDED SUGARLOAF CABBAGE WITH BURRATA & SPICED BUTTER

I love this dish. It came about as a mistake, trying to do a version of stuffed cabbage. I use sugarloaf cabbage because of its conical shape, sweet taste, and soft texture, but if it isn't available, you could use a small savoy cabbage. To add a little further edge to this dish, try grating some winter black truffle over it … YUM! **Serves 4 sharing**

INGREDIENTS

½ sugarloaf or savoy cabbage, finely shredded

1 tablespoon salt

2 burrata (see glossary) or soft mozzarella

3 tablespoons (40 g, 1½ oz) fresh breadcrumbs, toasted in the oven until golden

2 tablespoons pine nuts, toasted

1 small handful flat-leaf (Italian) parsley, washed and torn

1 tablespoon dried currants

SPICED BUTTER

1 cup plus 2 tablespoons (9 oz) unsalted butter, softened

5 garlic cloves, crushed

1 tablespoon chopped flat-leaf (Italian) parsley

good pinch of cayenne pepper

good pinch of ground turmeric

1 teaspoon capers, rinsed and chopped

1 teaspoon mustard powder (I use good old Keen's mustard powder)

4 anchovy fillets, chopped

zest and juice of 1 lemon

pinch of salt

METHOD

Put the cabbage in a bowl, mix with the salt, then leave to salt for 20 minutes. Rinse under cold running water to wash off the excess salt, then drain in a colander and set aside.

Combine all the spiced butter ingredients in a food processor. Add a pinch of salt, then blitz until it all comes together.

Layer the cabbage out over a large serving plate.

Now heat half the spiced butter in a saucepan until it crackles and turns a little brown. Dress the cabbage with the browned butter until it's all coated. Let sit a minute, then dress again to ensure all the cabbage is coated. (Any leftover butter can be sealed up and refrigerated for several weeks, or frozen for several months to use later.)

Tear the burrata all over the cabbage. In a bowl, quickly mix together the breadcrumbs, pine nuts, parsley, and currants, then scatter over the cabbage. Delicious.

We spoil ourselves with warming whiskeys and full-bodied red wines, and eating becomes an indulgence. We brew ourselves concoctions of ginger, honey, and lemon to protect our bodies from winter bugs.

SQUID, SCALLOPS & FENNEL WITH PEA & PROSCIUTTO DRESSING

Anyone from a certain time remembers a good old seafood salad. Well, this is my take on a more modern one. **Serves 4 as a starter or sharing, or 2 as a main course**

INGREDIENTS

2 squid, cut into rings; ask your fishmonger to clean and wash

8 small local scallops

salt to sprinkle

freshly ground black pepper

2 tablespoons (20 ml, 1 fl oz) good quality olive oil

juice of ½ lemon

1 small hot red or green chili, seeded and thinly sliced

1 fennel bulb, sliced wafer thin

crusty bread, to serve

PEA & PROSCIUTTO DRESSING

¼ cup (50 ml, 2 fl oz) olive oil

2 shallots, chopped

5 oz (140 g) thin slices prosciutto, torn into strips

1 cup frozen peas, thawed

1 small handful flat-leaf (Italian) parsley, washed and finely chopped

good pinch of sugar

METHOD

Using a sharp knife, slice the squid so it is wafer-thin—I have to say again, wafer-thin—think of small strips of paper, or dollar-bill thin. Place in a heatproof bowl that will fit over a pot. Tear the scallops into three or four small pieces and add to the squid.

To make the dressing, warm the olive oil, shallots and prosciutto in a saucepan over low heat. Once starting to brown a little, add the peas, parsley, sugar, and ½ cup (100 ml, 4 fl oz) water and bring to a boil. Cook for 2–3 minutes, until the peas are tender but not brown, and the liquid has turned into some nice pan juices. Take off the heat.

Bring a pot of water to a boil. Sprinkle the squid and scallops with salt and freshly ground black pepper. Add the olive oil and lemon juice, then place the bowl over the boiling pot, making sure the base of the bowl is not in contact with the water.

Using your fingers, keep mixing the seafood around for a minute or two, until the squid and scallops start to cook, but are still a little raw. Taste, check the seasoning, now take off the heat. Mix in the chili and fennel, then add all the dressing. Pile the salad onto serving dishes and eat warm.

This dish must be served with some crusty bread to mop up the juices on the plate ... and I would recommend always having some white wine with it!

NOTE: See the salad dressing family tree on page 232 for more wonderful ways to enjoy the Pea & Prosciutto Dressing.

WINTER

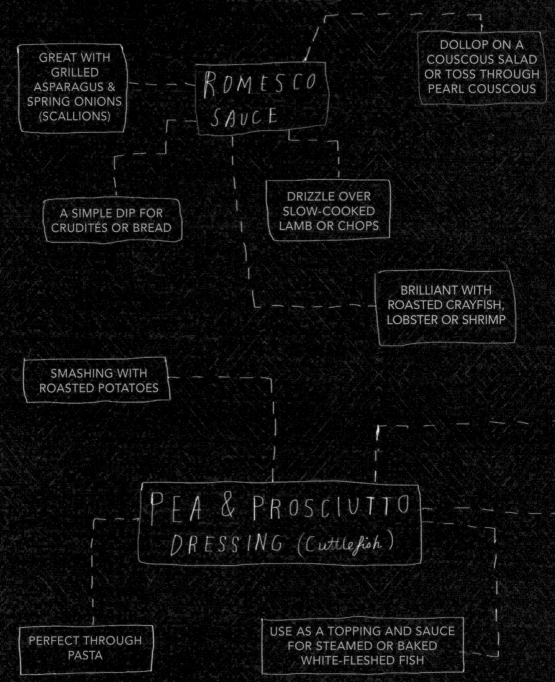

GREAT WITH GRILLED ASPARAGUS & SPRING ONIONS (SCALLIONS)

ROMESCO SAUCE

DOLLOP ON A COUSCOUS SALAD OR TOSS THROUGH PEARL COUSCOUS

A SIMPLE DIP FOR CRUDITÉS OR BREAD

DRIZZLE OVER SLOW-COOKED LAMB OR CHOPS

BRILLIANT WITH ROASTED CRAYFISH, LOBSTER OR SHRIMP

SMASHING WITH ROASTED POTATOES

PEA & PROSCIUTTO DRESSING (Cuttlefish)

PERFECT THROUGH PASTA

USE AS A TOPPING AND SAUCE FOR STEAMED OR BAKED WHITE-FLESHED FISH

SALAD DRESSING FAMILY TREE

WINTER

GREEN OLIVE DRESSING (Pumpkin & Falafel)
GREAT WITH ANY ROOT VEGGIES
MIX THROUGH A SIMPLE BOILED POTATO & EGG SALAD
USE LIKE A TAPENADE
DOLLOP OVER BARBECUED CALAMARI & ARGULA
SMEAR OVER ROASTED TOMATOES & ZUCCHINI
TOSS THROUGH A COLD PASTA SALAD
GREAT ON TOP OF TOASTED CIABATTA OR FOCACCIA; FOR A CHEEKY LITTLE LUNCH, ADD A POACHED EGG!
STIR THROUGH A PLAIN RISOTTO JUST BEFORE SERVING

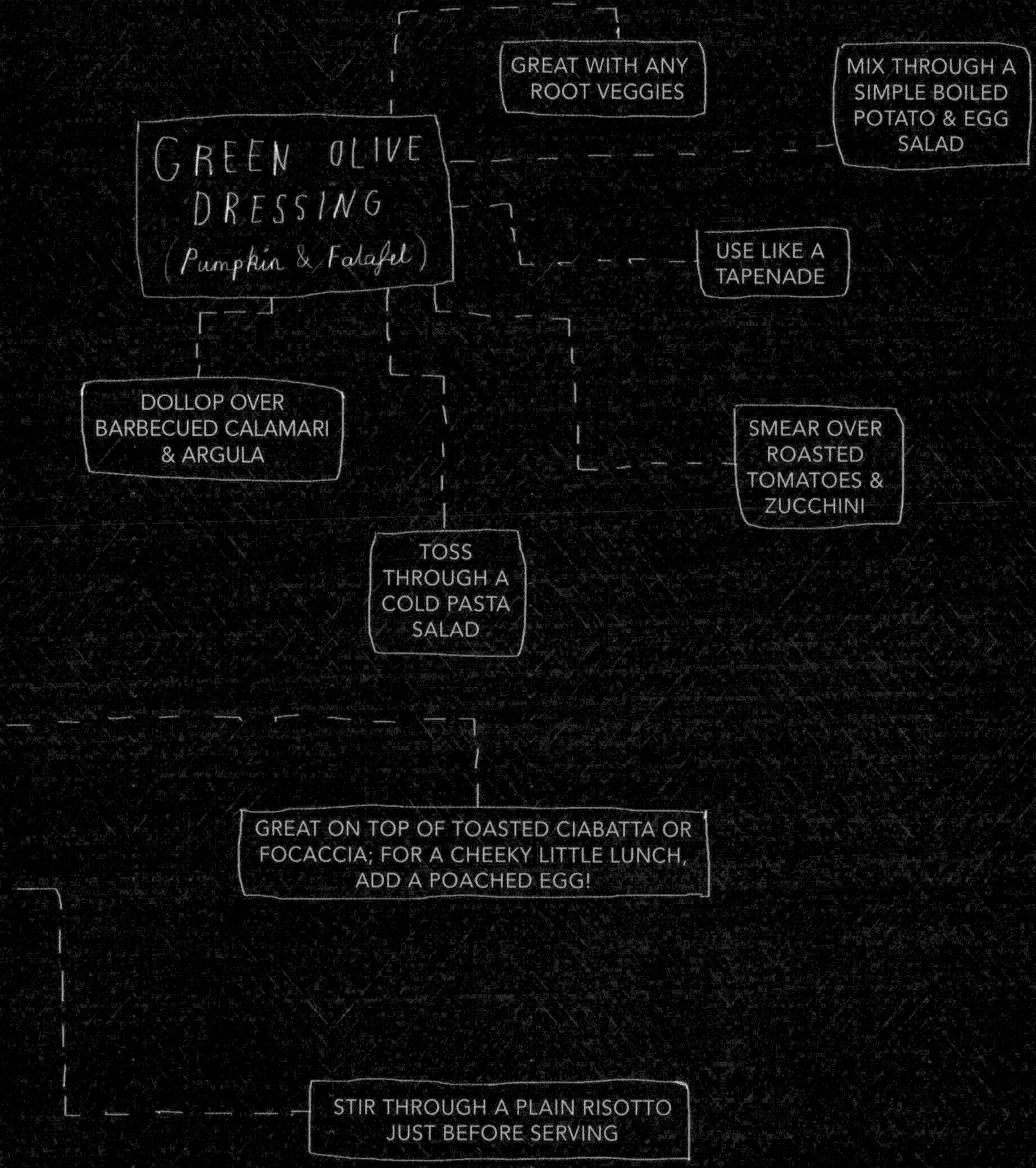

KIWI FRUIT & PAPAYA WITH LIME & CHILI

A refreshing salad in winter time with a hint of chili to spice up your life. **Serves 4**

INGREDIENTS

⅓ cup (75 g, 2¾ oz) superfine (caster) sugar

pinch of chili flakes

1 tablespoon rice wine vinegar

1 tablespoon vodka (optional)

zest and juice of 1 lime

4 kiwi fruit, peeled and cut into 8 wedges

½ ripe papaya, peeled, seeded, and diced

¾ cup plus 2 tablespoons (200 g, 7 oz) labneh (see glossary)

METHOD

In a small pot, bring the sugar, chili flakes, vinegar, vodka, if using, and ¼ cup (50 ml, 2 fl oz) water to a boil.

Stir in the lime juice and zest, take off the heat, and chill briefly.

Put the kiwi fruit and papaya in a mixing bowl, pour the chili syrup over and let sit for 5 minutes.

Place in serving bowls. Add a dollop of labneh and serve.

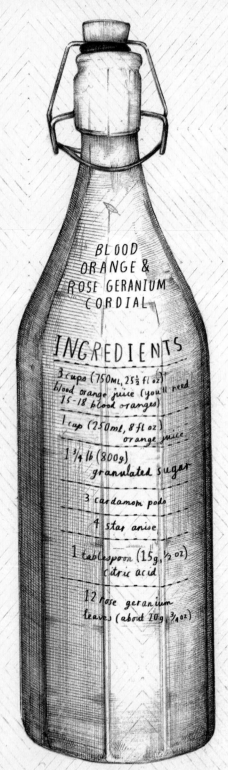

BLOOD
ORANGE &
ROSE GERANIUM
CORDIAL

INGREDIENTS

3 cups (750ML, 25½ fl oz)
blood orange juice (you'll need
15-18 blood oranges)

1 cup (250ML, 8 fl oz)
orange juice

1¾ lb (800g)
granulated sugar

3 cardamom pods

4 star anise

1 tablespoon (15g, ½ oz)
citric acid

12 rose geranium
leaves (about 20g, ¾ oz)

JASON'S AWARD-WINNING BLOOD ORANGE & ROSE GERANIUM CORDIAL

Jason, my daytime head chef at Pope Joan, loves making a cordial or two. From his concoctions, we always have a seasonal spritzer on the drinks menu at the Pope; he even makes them into ice pops during the warmer months. Cordials truly are a great way to capture a season in a bottle. Why they're award-winning, I'll leave to you to ask him if you happen to pop in to Pope Joan. **Makes about 5¼ cups (1¼ liters, 42½ fl oz)**

METHOD

Put all the ingredients except the rose geranium leaves in a large pot. Stir in 1 cup (250 ml, 8 fl oz) water and bring to a boil.

Reduce the heat and simmer for 10 minutes, then ladle off any impurities that have risen to the top.

Take off the heat and add the rose geranium leaves. Leave to infuse until cool, then strain into sterilized bottles and seal.

Keep in a cool dark place for up to 6 months. Once opened, store in the fridge and use within 8 weeks.

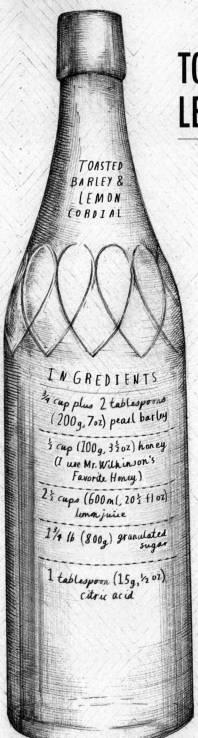

TOASTED BARLEY & LEMON CORDIAL

So, here is a different version from the lemon barley water on page 224. This cordial keeps longer, but I wouldn't use the barley again after using it in this recipe. **Makes 5¼ cups (1¼ liters, 42½ fl oz)**

METHOD

In a large pot, cook the barley over low heat for about 5–7 minutes, until it starts to turn a darkish golden color. Add the honey, then all the other ingredients. Pour in 4 cups (1 liter, 34 fl oz) water.

Increase the heat and bring to a boil, then reduce the heat to a simmer. Cook for 10 minutes, scooping off any impurities from the surface of the liquid.

Cool slightly, then strain into sterilized bottles and seal.

Keep in a cool dark place for up to 6 months. Once opened, store in the fridge and use within 4 weeks.

It is the end of the cycle—and also the beginning of the cycle—of life and of rebirth. For this reason the winter solstice, the shortest day of the year, is celebrated in many cultures across the world. This day is seen as a turning point from which the sun gets brighter and stronger as the year progresses.

BAHARAT SPICE BLEND "Baharat" translates as "spice" in Arabic. This is an all-purpose spice mix used in Middle Eastern cooking. Ingredients vary from region to region, but it commonly contains black pepper, coriander, paprika, nutmeg, cloves, cardamom, cumin, and cinnamon. You'll find it at your local Middle Eastern market or some supermarkets.

BILTONG A spiced, air-dried meat snack originating in South Africa, similar to beef jerky.

BLONDE SULTANAS Also known as "golden" or Iranian sultanas, these are lighter colored than regular sultanas because of the paler variety of grape used.

BOTTARGA Sometimes known as "poor man's caviar." This is a delicacy from Sardinia of salted and dried fish roe (usually mullet or tuna) that is thinly sliced and used as a condiment. You can make your own, but it's easy to find at a Mediterranean grocer.

BROWN KOSHI RICE Short for "koshihikari," koshi rice is a Japanese short-grain rice, considered the ultimate sushi rice for its texture and sweetness. This rice is less processed than its white counterpart with only the outermost layer (the "husk") removed.

BURRATA Italian for "buttery" or "buttered," burrata is a soft, fresh Italian cheese, made with an outer casing of mozzarella with a creamy, "buttery" oozing middle, giving it a gorgeous soft texture. Look for it in any good Mediterranean or cheese shop.

CHARDONNAY VINEGAR Made from chardonnay grapes. If you can't find chardonnay vinegar specifically, any good white wine vinegar is a suitable replacement.

CITRIC ACID An organic acid found in many fruits and veggies, especially citrus. It has a natural preservative quality and sour flavor. You'll find it in the baking aisle of your supermarket.

CORNICHONS A fancy French term for baby pickled cucumbers or gherkins.

FERMENTED BLACK BEANS These are Chinese black beans as opposed to the Mexican style. They are made from soy beans that have been dried and fermented with salt. You'll find them at your local Asian market.

FRISÉE Also known as curly endive and with a slightly bitter flavor, these salad leaves can be found seasonally at greengrocers.

GUANCIALE An Italian cured meat made from pork jowl or pork cheek.

LABNEH A strained yogurt, also known as "yogurt cheese." It is the curd that remains when excess water is drained from yogurt. You can make it yourself, or buy it from any Middle Eastern market or good cheese shop.

MÂCHE This tender, leafy salad green, highly popular in France, also goes by the names corn salad and lamb's lettuce. It is really delicious straight from the garden, so why not get some seeds and grow your own?

NIGELLA SEEDS Commonly used in Indian and Moroccan cuisines, these small black seeds are also known as black sesame, black cumin, black caraway, and black onion seed. They are sold in Indian and African grocers.

ORANGE FLOWER WATER Sometimes called orange blossom water, this is what it sounds like: the by-product of orange blossoms that have been distilled for their essential oil. It is used in both savory and sweet Middle Eastern foods, and really adds more of an aroma than a flavor.

PARMA HAM Another name for prosciutto; the salt-cured hind leg of a pig.

PIQUILLO PEPPER A sweet Spanish bell pepper (capsicum) variety with no heat. These are sold in cans at Spanish markets.

PURSLANE A succulent plant that is mostly considered a weed. You might have some growing in your garden. The leaves are crunchy with a slight salty flavor. Purslane is quite vitamin dense.

RAS EL HANOUT A Moroccan spice mix which translates to "top of the shop," in other words, the best spices available. For this reason there are many variations, but most blends include cardamom, nutmeg, anise, mace, cinnamon, ginger, various peppers, and turmeric.

RED MUSTARD LEAF The tasty leaves of the mustard plant, which belongs to the brassica family. The leaves have a slightly bitter flavor with a peppery bite. Your local greengrocer will be able to source them for you. Or you could grow your own!

SALT FLAKES The natural by-product of salt water evaporation. I prefer these as a natural flavor enhancer to the more highly processed and refined salt grains. There are some excellent salt flakes for culinary use.

SALTED RICOTTA Also called "ricotta salata," it is generally made from sheep's milk that has been pressed, salted, and aged for 90 days, producing a much firmer cheese than regular ricotta. Find it at good cheese shops or gourmet markets.

SAMPHIRE An edible succulent found in many coastal areas, also known as sea asparagus. It is crunchy with a salty flavor, lovely pickled or lightly blanched. You will find it seasonally at specialty grocers.

SHANKLISH A cheese from Syria and Lebanon, which may be made with either cow's or sheep's milk. It is generally sold in spheres the size of tennis balls, and can be fresh or aged. The more aged the shanklish, the stronger the flavor. Sold in Middle Eastern grocers.

SORREL This perennial herb looks a bit like spinach and has a distinct lemony flavor. Look for it at farmers' markets or greengrocers.

SUMAC A spice common to Middle Eastern dishes, made from dried and ground sumac berries. It has a sour astringent flavor a bit like lemon. Middle Eastern markets will have it.

VERJUICE/VERJUS The acidic juice of unripened, unfermented grapes or other tart fruit. It can be used in place of lemon juice or vinegar in recipes. It is sold in most supermarkets and specialty shops.

WATERMELON RADISH One of my favorite heirloom varieties of radish. It is white outside and bright pink on the inside, resembling a watermelon, hence the name. The flavor is similar to other radishes, which can be used as an alternative if your grocer can't source them. You could also grow your own. Radishes only take around three weeks from seed to crop—totally worth it!

WHITE ANCHOVIES Called "boquerones" in Spain, these anchovies have been marinated in oil and vinegar, and are completely different from the more common canned variety that you get on a pizza. They are sold fresh in good specialty shops or fish markets.

WHITE BALSAMIC VINEGAR Made from the "must" (pressed skins) of the white trebbiano grape variety. The vinegar is then cooked to produce its flavor, but unlike regular "dark" balsamic, it is cooked for a shorter period and at a lower temperature to ensure it retains its light color.

WHITE SESAME OIL The oil produced from white sesame seeds, which are lighter and more "floral" than their black counterparts. Stocked by Asian grocers.

Entries with an initial capital letter are recipes; lower case entries are general topics.

ACKNOWLEDGMENTS

Book number two, a sincere thanks to all from near and far. My family back in the United Kingdom, all of you, I hope I make you proud. To family and friends here, but especially Uncle Deano and Auntie Vanessa, thank you for the laughs, fun, food and for keeping the darts trophy safe in Queensland.

To my business partner, Ben (and Larissa, Frankie, and Alby), a special thank you. I love working with you, how we grow and what we have and what you stand for, and especially for being able to put up with my craziness. I truly hope we grow old in friendship and work together and reflect back in years just how good life is.

To the main people behind everything we do. Jason Newton you're a rock, bud, I'm at rest knowing you are in the kitchen; Vanessa Mateus, you are a rose, a shining rose, thank you for all your help getting the photos together for the book—and your endless work for us at Pope Joan. The rest of the team at Pope Joan, thank you for helping to make Pope Joan and Hams & Bacon special places to own and work in, with a special shout-out to Mark Hoba Paul, Adam, Rochelle, Fran, Bec, Rosanne, Jenni, Travis, and Jody.

To the most important people in food: all the farmers and producers I use. I can't name names in case I forget someone, but you know who you are. Thank you for teaching me, giving me advice, and just for producing some of the best food and service in the world. Good food comes down to you guys, so thank you for making my life so enjoyable and easy.

To everybody who worked amazingly on the book: Paul and Rachel from studio Racket, Stan (aka Miso), Brydie (aka Little Sister), Deb Kaloper, Jacqui Melville, Sonia Grieg, Katri Hilden, and the team behind Hardie Grant, Lucy, Paul (make sure the champagne keeps coming, bud), and Mark.

Thank you all from the bottom of my heart. I'm so proud of what we have achieved.

xxx